COMPOSTING

The Organic Natural Way

DICK KITTO

D1400306

THORSONS PUBLISHING GROUP

Revised edition 1987
Completely revised and expanded edition 1988

British Library Cataloguing in Publication Data

Kitto, Dick
Composting: the organic natural way—Rev. ed.
1. Compost
I. Title
635'.048975   S661

ISBN 0-7225-1588-X

*Published by Thorsons Publishers Limited,
Wellingborough, Northamptonshire, NN8 2RQ, England*

Printed in Great Britain by Woolnough Bookbinding,
Irthlingborough, Northamptonshire

1   3   5   7   9   10   8   6   4   2

CONTENTS

ACKNOWLEDGEMENTS

Thanks to Jane Harvey and Francis Blake of the Soil Association for their help with the appendix and to the Soil Association for permission to quote from their *Standards for Organic Agriculture*.

Thanks to Ashen Venema who took all the photographs for the book, bar the photograph of the compost bin on page 19, for which I thank Ron Allen.

Thanks also to Greenpeace and the Political Ecology Research Group for providing the information from which the map on page 120 was drawn.

INTRODUCTION

I wrote the first edition of this book in 1977. In those days I used to meet many gardeners, commercial growers and farmers and I even sometimes went to horticultural or farming conferences. If I was ever foolhardy enough to mention 'organic methods' I was treated with a mixture of jokey contempt and commiseration. I was regarded as a 'crank'.

What a change there has been in the intervening ten years! All the warnings and dire predictions that the organic movement were then uttering have suddenly come home to roost: agrochemicals are in the dock, anxieties about pesticides, nitrate pollution of rivers, soil compaction, soil erosion, destruction of the environment, overproduction, are all here in Britain, now, and the powers-that-be have been forced, tardily, to take notice.

I end this book now as I did then with the sentence 'The day of reckoning may be closer than we think.' That has proved true, and it is still true because, as with all bureaucracies, reaction is slow, bewildered and half-hearted, whereas what is needed to avert a world-wide environmental catastrophe is action that is urgent and decisive.

So when you make compost, when you garden organically, you are not just growing fresh, pesticide-free vegetables for yourself, you are part of a growing movement for change. And if there are still people around who call you a 'crank', remember the memorable words of E. F. Schumacher: 'Some people call me a crank. I don't mind that at all. A crank is a low-cost, low-capital, non-violent tool and it makes revolutions.'

But there is something else as well. Here are some more memorable words, this time from the Thorpe report on allotments: 'allotment holdings provide a healthy physical recreation for people of all ages and occupations, especially for those living in a crowded urban environment. It affords relaxation from the stresses of modern life and yet is also creative. It involves the use of numerous mental stimuli, powers of observation and planning, appraisals of beauty in form, scent and colour, the love of nature and the mystique of growing things'.

Gardening, nurturing plants that are healthy, providing food, feeding the waste products back to increase the fertility of the soil, participating in this age-old process by which the whole of the living world has grown and continues to survive, satisfies our inborn instinct for creativity in a way that few other activities can do. There is a sense of wholeness and wholesomeness about it that makes us look with awe at the way our present civilization spreads its asphalt and cement remorselessly over the green countryside, and sprays the remainder with poisons and pollutants.

A central step in this natural cycle of

operations is the returning of waste organic material to the soil, and the present interest in compost is only a rediscovery of what has been practised since time immemorial.

Like many of the ways in which the human race has attempted to better its lot on this earth, the principles of composting are derived from observation of natural processes. When waste organic matter is left under natural conditions it will begin to decompose as the result of the action of various organisms. These are chiefly microbial but worms, slugs, small animals and birds also play their part. In theory this decomposition could continue over the years until the organic matter is completely mineralized, but in normal circumstances this never happens though it comes near to it when organic matter under waterlogged conditions turns into peat and peat into lignite or coal.

At an intermediate stage in this process of decomposition the organic matter becomes compost; this stage is very difficult to define chemically or biologically but relatively easy to recognize in practice by the fact that the material becomes dark brown, fibrous, reasonably homogeneous and has a characteristic clean earthy smell. It is at this stage that, mixed with soil already existing, it becomes an ideal medium for the growth of plants.

This process has been going on naturally for millenia, slowly building up the fertility of the soil; it is in fact, together with the breaking down of the original rock into particles under the action of the weather, the process by which all soil is formed and on which all natural vegetation and therefore all life depends. The compost heap is a device by which the natural process is concentrated and speeded up to cater for the extra demands of intensive growing. By confining large quantities of organic matter into a relatively small space under optimum conditions, the speed and efficiency of decomposition is increased so that large quantities of compost can be produced in a short time.

The compost heap is thus an artificial phenomenon, nowhere to be found in nature. In this respect it is no different from all the other operations of agriculture and horticulture: they are all interferences in natural processes and in the natural rhythm of growth and decay; they are all attempts by the human race to swing the ecological balance in its favour. All animals are engaged in a similar struggle for survival; the human race is unique in the intelligence and ingenuity it brings to bear on this struggle, in the scale of its activities and more recently in its ruthlessness.

The organic movement has always stood against many of these trends, and others are beginning to have their doubts. Are modern methods of chemical food production the only or the best ones to meet present day demands? And if they are, may they not be building up problems for future generations which they will be unable to solve?

What we as compost gardeners are aiming to do is not to return to wholly natural conditions, which obviously would be those of the forest and the jungle, but to work sufficiently in harmony with natural processes to establish our own place securely within the existing environment.

This book is about compost: how to make it, how to use it, and at the same time how to relate what we are doing to the long-term fruitfulness of the soil which still remains, as it always has been, the basis on which the health and stability of our civilization depends.

I think there is one thing that needs to be emphasized at the very start, and never to be forgotten: making compost is a simple, natural process. It is going on all the time, in the hedgerows, in the ditches, beneath the grassland, in the forest. Whatever the conditions, nature adapts and the process goes on. It goes on in your kitchen compost bucket, in your gardens, in your compost heap. Anyone who has to do with food will know that it is almost impossible to stop the decomposition of living matter, short of freezing it, sterilizing it or dehydrating it.

The cycle of birth, growth, death and decay is one of the most inevitable laws of nature and whatever you do nature will be on your side and will come to your rescue. So do not be put off by the experts who say 'Oh, you should have done this or that'; do not worry if your compost heap will not heat up, or smells funny, or seems to be waterlogged. None of these things is a total disaster and even if you do nothing about them you will still get compost of a sort eventually.

In this book, I have tried to cover the whole process fairly thoroughly, and at first glance this may give the impression that it is all very complicated and you must follow instructions exactly. But that is not the case.

What is true is that the more you understand and the more careful you are the better your compost will be and the quicker you will get it. But do not be downhearted if things do not go right the first time. Do not be flustered by complicated instructions and advice. Take it easy; learn by stages; do what seems sensible; work with nature, and nature will work with you.

CHAPTER 1
BASIC PRINCIPLES OF COMPOST MAKING

If you are in the habit of reading gardening books you will find that there are several different and often contradictory views on the best way to make compost. For instance Sir Albert Howard, originator of the 'Indore method', upon which so much of modern compost lore and practice is based, and the first person in modern times to apply an analytical and scientific approach to the subject, tells us to make our heap in a shallow pit. This is doubtless because he originated his method in India where the climate is dry and moisture has to be conserved. But if you live on the western foothills of the Pennines you will be told to build on a mound so as to drain off some of the 70 to 80 in (180-200 cm) of rainfall that falls each year.

The important thing is the knowledge not only of what to do, but the reasons for doing it, so that you can modify your methods to suit your particular circumstances.

Aerobic and Anaerobic
Basic to this knowledge is the understanding that there are two methods of composting which superficially are very similar to each other, in that they both involve piling organic matter in heaps in order to aid its decomposition. But they are very different in the way they operate, and this unrecognized difference is one of the causes of much failure and disappointment. The first method is the one which is described or implied in almost all books on the subject, in which the decomposition results mainly from the action of bacteria that require oxygen and that flourish within a temperature range 120° to 150°F (48° to 65°C). These bacteria breed and work very fast and, given the right conditions, will produce usable compost in a month. This method is often described as being 'aerobic', meaning it requires a free flow of air (oxygen), and 'thermophilic', meaning it operates at a high temperature. The second method is one where the bacteria do not require oxygen, and do not generate heat. This method is very much slower and normally takes about a year to produce good compost. It is usually described as being 'anaerobic', meaning that it does not require air or oxygen. The words 'aerobic' and 'anaerobic' are rather cumbersome, but they are so convenient and so widely understood that it is difficult to avoid using them. I shall therefore use them throughout this book: aerobic will refer principally to a compost heap in which aeration plays a major part; it can also refer to the process of decomposition in such a heap, to the bacteria that cause the decomposition and to the resulting compost. 'Anaerobic' refers to a heap where aeration does not occur, and also to the bacteria and processes that operate in this case.

The majority of compost heaps are

aimed at the aerobic method, and perhaps achieve it for a short period; but either from the beginning, or after the first few days, change to being anaerobic.

Undoubtedly the aerobic method has many advantages and produces the better compost. On the other hand it is more difficult, and takes a lot more trouble; and there are certainly occasions when the anaerobic is a simpler and perfectly adequate method.

We have then a choice as to which method to use and before trying to make it we need to look carefully at the two alternatives so that we have some facts and understanding on which to base a comparison.

The Aerobic Method

Before considering the detailed requirements of the aerobic compost heap it is as well to describe briefly the operation as a whole. The main workers in this process are the bacteria*, literally billions of millions of them, of many thousands of different species. The requirements of the bacteria are very much the same as our own: food, air, moisture, warmth. As soon as they find themselves in conditions that provide these requirements they begin to breed; once started they breed very fast and the population increases dramatically. This creates energy in the form of heat, and the heap starts to warm up; the original species of bacteria find the going too hot and die off, to be replaced by new species, the thermophilic bacteria, which flourish in these higher temperatures. The plant food is consumed, transformed, excreted and recycled. Many different species of bacteria move in as the temperature rises still further.

To us humans this is a familiar scene: it is a growth economy gone mad, a rising population making more and more demands on the limited resources

of their little world of the compost heap: there is bound to be a reckoning. The limiting factor, as perhaps in our own society, is the demand for energy. For the energy of the heap, which manifests itself as heat, comes from the combination of the carbon in the plant materials and the oxygen in the air that fills the pore spaces: slowly but inevitably the oxygen is used up in the process to be replaced by carbon dioxide, and the spectre of suffocation looms ahead; unmindful, the bacteria continue their breeding; but it is no good: the end is near. The pore spaces are clogged, the great food reserves of carbon lie untouched by the oxygen-starved bacteria, the temperature falls; the cycle is complete.

Now there advances upon this scene of desolation the bacterial vultures – the anaerobic bacteria. The lack of oxygen does not worry them, it is to their advantage for now they have the field to themselves; they can take their time as they methodically colonize this little universe and prepare for the long year's haul ahead.

The rise and fall of this compost civilization will have taken less than a week and its progress can be measured by anyone with a silage thermometer, for it runs parallel with the rise and fall

*I use the term 'bacteria' here, though in fact a variety of organisms are involved, including fungi, actinomycetes, viruses, algae and protozoae. Some writers use the word 'micro-organisms', but this isn't strictly accurate either, as some of them such as protozoae are comparatively large. Also it is rather a clumsy mouthful to keep repeating. The word 'organism', also often used, is confusing too: it can refer to anything from an amoeba to an elephant. So I shall stick to 'bacteria', using it in its dictionary sense of 'microscopic organism' rather than its scientific one.

of the temperature. If this is plotted on a graph, it will look something like this:

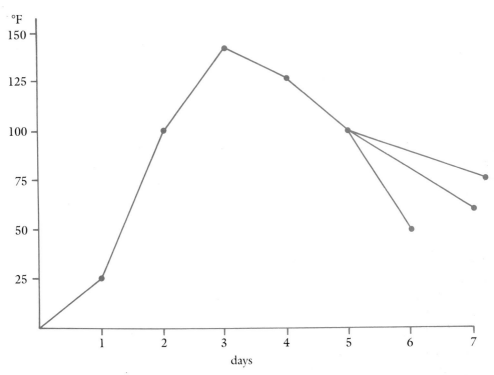

The speed of decline of temperature after day 5 will depend on the insulation properties of the heap, but one can expect that it will fall in a gradual curve and after about three weeks the heap will have reverted to roughly the temperature of the surrounding soil.

This, then, is a picture of how a well-made heap, initially aerobic, will very rapidly become anaerobic – an inevitable process unless steps are taken to counteract it. The key factor is obvious: it is the shortage of oxygen. And so if you wish to maintain a rapid, high-temperature, aerobic heap, you must allow the suffocating carbon dioxide to escape, open out the pore spaces and replenish them once more with life-giving oxygen. The most straightforward way of doing this is to turn the heap, and as soon as you do this the whole life cycle begins again.

If you study this cycle it is clear what environmental conditions you should aim at:

Food

This is the composition of the materials that go to make the heap. There must be a variety of this to sustain life. Bacteria do not live on carbon and oxygen alone but require a wide variety of nutrients just as other animals do. A shortage of carbon is not in normal circumstances likely to be a limiting factor, except perhaps in the case of a pile entirely composed of soft, sappy, green material (e.g. lawn mowings). Apart from oxygen, the commonest shortage is of nitrogen, another essential ingredient of living things (the whole question of nitrogen content will receive special attention in the next section).

Moisture

There must be as much moisture as possible, but never so much that the pore spaces become waterlogged. In other words, the compost heap must be damp but not wet.

Heat

The heap must be enabled to heat up, and this involves some form of insulation.

Air

Providing these first three conditions are correct, the limiting factor is aeration, and to maintain this is the major requirement for aerobic decomposition.

We will now turn to these four requirements and consider them in turn in a little more detail.

Composition of Materials

Anything that has lived will make compost, but some things are better than others. For example, pine needles are unsuitable because they contain a resin that is detrimental to the growth of most plants. Dead pigs are unsuitable because they are illegal – a few years ago a farmer was prosecuted for having a dead pig in his manure heap. Most people know that if you make a heap entirely of grass mowings it will produce nothing but a slimy black mass. If you make a heap entirely of broccoli stalks the end product will still be broccoli stalks. What is needed is a mixture, but even then some care is needed in selecting the ingredients.

The principle criterion for this selection is the proportion of carbon and nitrogen in the materials. Both these elements are essential to the life of bacteria, and the proportion between them is a critical factor. All animal and vegetable matter contain both of them in varying concentrations. In general,

carbon is present in woody matter, hard stalks and roots; nitrogen is concentrated in the leaf and green part of the plant, and also in the little white nodules to be found on the roots of leguminous plants – peas, beans, clovers and vetches.

The amount of carbon and nitrogen in the original organic matter should be roughly in the proportion of 30:1, which during the process of decomposition will reduce to about 10:1. This reduction comes about because, as already explained, a proportion of the carbon combines with oxygen to produce energy in the form of heat and is released as carbon dioxide waste, in exactly the same way as we consume carbohydrates and oxygen and breathe out carbon dioxide. If there is too much carbon, decomposition will be slowed down and the correct temperature will not be reached. If there is too much nitrogen this will be lost and wasted. As the ratio 30:1 is rather meaningless to most people I have prepared the list opposite as a guide.

In selecting materials you should attempt to maintain a balance between the number of carbon crosses and the number of nitrogen crosses. For instance, if you have a lot of wheat straw (XXX carbon) you should try to balance it with an equal quantity of, say, poultry droppings (XXX nitrogen) or a larger quantity of comfrey (XX nitrogen), and so on. This table, by the way, shows why the combination of cow dung and straw is such a satisfactory one, as they balance each other with high proportions of carbon and nitrogen. However, in farm heaps there is often a tendency for the proportion of dung to be too great, with a consequent loss of nitrogen in the form of ammonia, which accounts for the pungent smell given off in the early stages.

Luckily for us nature is very accom-

CARBON-NITROGEN RATIO IN COMPOST			
	N	*C*	*Remarks*
Urine	XXXX		Potash
Dried Blood	XXXX		
Fish Waste	XXX		Phosphates
Poultry Manure	XXX		Phosphates; very 'hot'
Cow Manure	XXX		Without straw
Lawn Mowings	XX		
Comfrey	XX		Potash
Pomace	XX		
Hops	XX		
Tomato Haulms	XX	X	
Pig Manure	XX		Cold
Farmyard Manure	XXX	XX	Including straw as usually found (fresh)
Seaweed	XX	X	Potash (varies a little)
Legume Tops	XX		
Legume Whole	XX	X	
Pea and Bean Haulms	XX		
Horse Manure	XX	X	Including straw
Fern	X	X	Potash, if cut green
Peat	X	X	
Oat Straw	X	XX	
General Garden Weeds	X	XX	
Newspaper		XX	
Wheat Straw		XXX	
Woody Stems, Hard Brassica Stalks		XXX	
Sawdust		XXXX	

modating and is determined to make all things grow (think of the 1,000,000,000 spermatozoa to produce one baby!) so there is no need to keep to these quantities accurately; they are a guide only, but the nearer you keep to them the better compost you will make.

Another important factor is size of material: obviously the bacteria mainly attack the surface of the material so that large pieces with a low ratio of surface to volume are slow to decompose. In addition the surface often consists of a hard protective layer which acts as a barrier to the more easily decomposed matter beneath. It is therefore important that large pieces of material should be chopped up as small as possible – the surface area of a brassica stalk is roughly trebled if it is chopped into pieces one inch long.

A third factor is the chemical quality of the carbon compounds, for some of these are far more resistant to decay than others. Even in the form of sawdust, many woods will take well over two years to decay into compost, and will require a large supply of nitrogen to do so. It is important to be very cautious about incorporating such materials into a compost heap that you expect to use within this time. The employment of sawdust as a surface mulch is a controversial subject which will be discussed later.

Particularly to be avoided is manure based on wood chippings, which is becoming increasingly common in areas where straw is hard to come by. Of course wood chippings will eventually break down to make good compost but it is likely to take a very long time and, if used prematurely, will certainly cause serious nitrogen starvation (see page 63).

Aeration

As already explained, the life-style of microbes is self-destructive because in using up the available oxygen they release in its place carbon dioxide which fills the pore spaces previously occupied by air. In other words they suffocate themselves by over-breeding in a limited environment. This can happen very rapidly. A heap will usually rise to maximum activity and begin to decline again within five days.

Much of the technology of large-scale composting is directed toward aeration, usually by means of some form of continuous agitation or turning and mixing, and this emphasizes the key importance of this operation. There is no doubt that *continuous* turning provides the quickest and most efficient way of making good compost and that the nearer you approach this ideal the better things will be. Unfortunately there is no substitute for turning, and most of the other suggestions proposed for improving aeration are more or less useless, if not actually detrimental. However I think it worth while to take a look at a few of these suggestions, if only to save people labour and disappointment.

Some people advocate putting lines of bricks along the bottom of the heap to create air channels. Others propose building the heap on a wire mesh. These proposals, with appropriate diagrams, work well in books, but are not entirely trouble-free when it comes to actually making the heap.

How, for instance, are you actually going to get the compost out at the end? The normal and undoubtedly the best way to shovel anything is to slide your spade or shovel along at floor level – and how can you do this if you go slap bang into a line of bricks or get entangled in a mesh of wire netting?

But there is another factor; these methods are ineffective because, as the bacteria gnaw and nibble away at the organic matter, masticate it, metabolize it, digest it, excrete it, they diminish its bulk (just as we do when we eat lettuces and endives and chicory and excrete little brown compact sausages) and this causes the whole mass of the compost heap to compact down, forming an airtight mass which no amount of wire mesh can aerate.

Much the same comments are applicable to plunging iron pipes in from the top to form air vents: experience has shown that even pipes pumping forced air through vents have not been very successful because the air penetrates so unevenly and not far enough.

Another method advocated is to make the sides of the bin slatted, so that air can penetrate inwards through the heap. Again, it is extremely doubtful whether this will succeed in its object, but even if it does to a small extent you

are coming up against a problem of insulation, because the purpose of the container is principally to insulate the heap, and if you leave gaps in it this will obviously cut down its insulating properties. In addition, the flow of air through the slats will cause the surface of the heap to dry out at these points and almost no decomposition will take place.

In fact the demand for aeration is incompatible with the demand for insulation, and although it is the need for aeration that is the most important of these, by this method you are getting very little of the former at a considerable loss of the latter.

The experience of nearly all compost makers has demonstrated that, if you wish to maintain your compost heap in an aerated condition, the only sure method is to turn it as frequently as

This is a photograph of a compost bin at the Royal Horticultural Society's gardens at Wisley. As you would expect it is very well made, but its design is based on the belief that slatted sides provide aeration. This idea has now been overtaken by more modern methods and I believe that this bin has now been replaced.

possible. How frequently you turn is rather up to you, and will be discussed further under the mixed aerobic/anaerobic section; but if you want to obtain the *maximum* aerobic efficiency you should aim to turn your heap every three or four days, in which case, other things being well, you should produce compost in about twelve days, that is with three turns. But do not worry; it is not in the least *essential* to turn your heap this often; I am only stating the way to get the quickest results – a doctrine of perfection that very few people manage to achieve or, for that matter, need to.

There is now on the market a compost bin that can be rotated. This is an adaptation for domestic use of a system that is used in many large-scale composting plants. The bin is rather small and is, therefore, suitable mainly for the small garden. I have not tried it but reports on it seem to be fairly positive. Some people have complained that the resulting compost tends to become too wet and slimy, so it is evidently important to incorporate plenty of dry material into the mixture. Don't forget that most vegetation and kitchen wastes are 90 per cent or more water so what seems only moderately damp when you put it in may become saturated as it decomposes.

Moisture

The amount of moisture present is very important, for bacteria cannot flourish in dry conditions. Equally, aerobic bacteria will be drowned in over-wet conditions, though of course anaerobic decomposition will occur even in a completely waterlogged state: that, as already mentioned, is how peat is formed, but the process takes several thousands of years. The difference in rainfall between the east and the west of England, and to a lesser extent between winter and summer, is sufficient to affect the process profoundly, and must be taken into account when making the heap. The only reliable way of controlling the amount of moisture present is to protect the heap from variations in weather conditions, and provide the water artificially.

This, then, is one good reason for containing the heap in a box and putting a roof on it. It is also a good reason against starting it off in a pit, unless you are building it on a soil that is very porous indeed.

In fact, protecting it against water-logging from below is almost as important as protecting it against flooding from above. If your soil is at all heavy it is worth building the heap in a slightly raised position and leaving gaps at the bottom of the walls to ensure that it keeps well drained and dried out at the bottom (note that these gaps are nothing to do with aeration).

Temperature

The artificiality of an aerobic compost heap is most noticeably manifested in the temperature it reaches. Natural decomposition rarely results in a rise in temperature beyond a very few degrees, so that throughout the duration of the process roughly consistent conditions prevail and roughly the same micro-organisms will operate. In an aerobic compost heap, on the other hand, the rapid increase in temperature gives rise to quite a different class of organism (the thermophilic bacteria) and it is interesting to speculate on the fact that these organisms, absent under natural conditions, nevertheless occur spontaneously when the conditions that suit them arise. Where do they come from? Where have they been lurking all these thousands of millions of years, waiting, as it were, in ambush for man to invent the first compost heap?

These organisms, whose occurrence is so intriguing and inexplicable, represent a lucky break for gardeners, for they enable the good composter to achieve two important results: the destruction of weed seeds and perennial roots; and the destruction of pathogenic bacteria. Both of these certainly occur with a temperature of 150°F (65°C) but also happen almost as effectively with a damp temperature of 120°F (49°C) lasting over a period of several days.

A temperature of somewhere between 120° and 150°F (49°-65°C) represents a goal for composters which is hard to achieve. For, whereas the other factors mentioned – composition, aeration and moisture – are largely under our control, temperature is not. The correct temperature occurs naturally when the other conditions are right, or at least it should do so. Sometimes, inexplicably, it does not and then the composter is stumped, because if the temperature has not risen, then the bacteria are not breeding, and that means the compost is not working and there is very little he can do but start again.

Insulation

The principal way in which we can improve the situation is by ensuring that the heap is insulated. In a very large heap the outside layers act as an insulation barrier for the inner layers; but there is a minimum size below which the heat losses from the surface are so great that the heap will never heat up sufficiently, however well made it is in other respects and however much activity the bacteria engender. This size is in the region of 6 by 6 by 5 ft (2 by 2 by 1.5m) high and so is beyond the reach of the ordinary small gardener or allotment holder.

For smaller heaps some sort of insulation has to be provided, normally in the form of a bin or box. Here again there is still a minimum size below which even a boxed-in heap will not retain enough heat, and this is usually taken to be a 3 or 4 ft (1 or 1.25m) cube, though this depends very much on the climate. The heat losses on an exposed part of the north west of Scotland are very different from those in a south-facing garden in Torquay.

The Question of Size

This question of size poses one of the major and largely unacknowledged problems for the small gardener. For the reality of his situation is that his main compost ingredients, kitchen refuse and garden waste, come in small quantities every day or so, and so it is only after a considerable period that its quantity builds up to enough to make a reasonable sized heap. What he tends to do is to put material on the heap as it comes so that in its vital early stages of decomposition it never attains the critical size to enable the temperature to build up. Thus the initial phases of bacterial activity which should have been raising the temperature to thermophilic conditions are, from this point of view, largely wasted.

One solution to this is to form a co-operative composting arrangement with neighbours, so that one weekend, say, enough material can be gathered together to fill one member's heap to the top, and the next weekend the next person's heap is filled and so on. I have heard of arrangements like this but have never actually come across one in practice.

The other method does not involve neighbours and will be described in chapter 2.

The Anaerobic Method

This is the method that is familiar, for

instance, in heaped turf, where inverted turves are stacked and left for about twelve months to become 'turf loam', a basic ingredient of John Innes Potting Compost. It is also familiar in many compost heaps that have not maintained their initial aeration.

It is, in fact, similar to the 'earth compost' with which the Chinese maintained the fertility of their soil over such long periods. China is a large country and so several different methods of composting were used in different areas, but it is clear that 'earth compost' and similar anaerobic systems were one of the commonest. The heaps were made in the open, often just outside the house or even in the village street, usually 4 to 5 ft (1.22-1.5m) high and sometimes very large. When completed they were clad in a 2 to 3in (5-8cm) layer of soil which was beaten hard. They usually incorporated large quantities of earth, especially of alluvial mud from river banks or streams, which was very fertile, and also clover and other green manure crops grown especially for the purpose. In addition they would include their own (human) manure. Nowadays most people would be chary of including this in an anaerobic heap (but see pages 49-50) and if they used it at all would limit its use to aerobic heaps that will heat up sufficiently to sterilize any pathogenic bacteria. The Chinese evidently did not take this precaution, but we do not know whether they suffered illness as a result. The use of night soil (urine) in an anaerobic heap or directly on the soil is, however, perfectly safe.

When the heap had decomposed, before carting the compost out to the fields, they would in many cases spread it on the ground to dry out, pulverize it and then leave it to mature for several weeks*.

The anaerobic method will not des-troy perennials, so it is important to exclude these. In theory it is possible to chop them up, hammer and crush them and lay them out in the sun to wither and die; but it is much safer to put them on the 'rough heap' (see page 59) or burn them and use the ash. Nor will it kill weed seeds or pathogenic bacteria, so anything liable to go putrid should be excluded – animal or fish waste, for example. Manure may be used provided it is covered up, though, as will be explained later, it is wasteful to use fresh manure in an anaerobic heap when it could be used as an activator for an aerobic one.

Apart from this the anaerobic heap has few limitations and restrictions. Naturally bacterial activity will slow down during cold weather and in fact will more or less come to a halt during a hard winter, so even here there is an advantage in 'boxing in' the heap. In any case it is advisable to cover the heap so that it does not cause a nuisance. You can follow Chinese practice and cover your heap with an earth cladding or use old carpets, felt or, at a pinch, plastic sheeting. Again, the degree of moisture is not nearly so critical, although it is important to make sure that the heap is not allowed to get too dry. The main danger is that uncovered heaps get very wet and cold during the winter, when

*This information was gleaned from *Farms of Forty Centuries* by F. H. King (first published in 1911 but has since been reissued by Rodale Press Inc., Book Division, Emmaus, Pennsylvania 18049, U.S.A.), a little-known but fascinating account of a tour of Chinese, Japanese and Korean food-producing areas. I understand, mainly from newspaper articles that, since this time, China has followed the West by introducing 'agro-chemical' methods but, because of erosion and other problems is now having second thoughts, as we are.

they will putrefy rather than decompose.

That is about all there is to it. The process will take about a year, and the end product may well have quite a lot of rough material mixed in it. It is liable also to be rather sticky, and may be too acid. The best procedure is to fork it over, remove the rough material to pass on to the next heap, loosen and aerate what is left, apply lime, and leave it to mature in the open for about a month before using.

Generally speaking the anaerobic heap has received a very rough deal from composters, but it has many advantages: in particular it is useful for the production of turf loam, which, quite apart from its use in John Innes compost, is a valuable form of composted soil. It is also satisfactory for rough heaps, for large quantities of rough grass, straw and the like, and for material that has a lot of soil in it. Before attempting to make any final choice between the two methods it is worth listing their comparative advantages and disadvantages (see the table on the following page).

The Mixed Heap

There is no reason why these two methods should not be combined and this is probably the best choice for the person who has limited time at his disposal. Let us look at how most people operate their compost heaps.

As materials come to hand they are deposited in the compost bin over a period of a couple of months or so. This happens very unevenly. After a weekend of gardening there are a lot of weeds; once a week or perhaps once a month the chicken shed is cleaned out and there's a layer of straw and manure; or there may be a party and a whole lot of kitchen waste appears. But in any case, for most of the time, the size of this heap will be below the critical size for proper thermophilic decomposition.

If the mixture is about right aerobic activity will start, but the temperature will never build up because of the surface losses, the oxygen will be used up, and anaerobic decomposition will set in. If the building of the heap is spread over not too long a period there will certainly be some rise in temperature before it settles into a gradual anaerobic decline. What has prevented the proper initial build-up of aerobic activity has been the fact that, because the partial heap was not large enough to retain and build up the heat, this was dissipated gradually over too long a period.

If at this stage, that is when a complete binful of material has accumulated, the heap is turned, then a fair amount of aerobic activity will follow and a fair heat will be achieved before it reverts to its anaerobic state. Failure results partly because people mistakenly expect a heap to remain heated and active over a long period without attention, which is both theoretically and practically impossible, and partly because the slow build-up of the heap in the early stages allows too much of the initial energy to be dissipated. Of course there are other possible reasons for failure connected with the ingredients and other factors, but assuming that these are more or less correct there are three choices open to the compost makers:

To eliminate all perennial weeds, animal and other obnoxious materials, and burn them on the bonfire, and opt for a trouble-free anaerobic heap with a through-put of about twelve months.

To aim for an aerobic heap and be prepared for turning at least twice, with a through-put of one or two months.

Aerobic	Anaerobic
Requires quite careful , preparation and continual attention	Requires very little preparation or attention
Can include almost any organic material	Must not include perennial weeds or hard materials
Normally requires boxing in or containing in a bin	Does not need boxing or containing
Must be of a minimum size	Can be any size
Requires turning	Does not require turning
Produces compost in one to two months (depending on the season)	Takes about a year to produce compost
Will kill all weed-seeds, and most perennial roots	Does not kill weed-seeds or perennial roots
Kills all pathogenic bacteria, does not produce odours or flies or other vermin	May produce odours, and flies, so should be carefully covered over
Produces a compost that is fairly homogenous and of about the right degree of acidity and ready for immediate use	May produce a rather cold, heavy compost, rather too acid, with some uncomposted fragments, which will require sieving before use
Does not require liming	Probably requires liming
Requires careful attention to carbon/nitrogen ratio, i.e. is likely to require an activator	Does not require such careful attention to carbon/nitrogen ratio although the larger the proportion of nitrogen, the quicker the heap will decompose to form compost

To settle for a mixed process, which is a combination of these two, and is really a rationalization of what most people actually do, or attempt to do. In the early stages whilst the quantity of material is being built up until there is enough to make a minimum-sized heap, conditions fluctuate unpredictably between aerobic and anaerobic. The heap is then built, decomposes aerobically, is possibly turned after a week or so, and then allowed to revert to anaerobic conditions, in which it remains until ready. This process would take two to three months during the summer and rather longer during the winter.

It seems to me that this method is the one best suited to most gardeners' needs, and it is the one I shall describe in the next chapter.

CHAPTER 2
PRACTICAL COMPOSTING

The Compost Area

It is hard to be dogmatic about the space you need for making compost because this depends on so many factors: how committed a compost maker you are, what method you use, how much space you have available, how much compost you aim to produce (and this again depends on the size of your garden, what you want to grow, what sort of soil you have and how fertile it is).

To start with I am going to make an assumption: that you should aim to produce the equivalent of a layer of compost between 1in and 2in (2.5-5cm) deep on your garden annually. This may seem rather a lot but my observations lead me to think that a great many vegetable gardens are under-fertilized. If you take over a new garden or allotment that is in poor heart, you will certainly need at least this amount initially. But I also think that quite a lot of compost and manure is used wastefully and in Chapter 3 I suggest ways in which it can be applied more economically. Let us for the moment accept an average figure of a 1½in (4cm) deep layer (you can reduce this if you feel it is more than your garden needs, and if you find it is more than you can manage to produce you can follow some of the suggestions in Chapter 3 for economizing).

Compost is a rather variable and unpredictable material and it is not possible to give exact measurements, but the following information should be taken as a rough and ready average:

1. As explained in the last chapter, there is a minimum size for a compost heap that will break down effectively, and this is usually given as being a 3 to 4ft (0.9-1.2m) cube. There is, however, a larger difference between these sizes than appears – a 4ft (1.2m) cube will make 2½ times as much usable compost as a 3ft (0.9m) cube. With well-made compost an initial 3ft (0.9m) high heap will quickly compact down to 2 feet (0.6m) high and in my experience a 3 by 3 by 2ft (0.9 by 0.9 by 0.6m) heap is too small an amount to work satisfactorily. Also, if you take into account the fact that the outer 6in (15cm) of any heap is unlikely to break down completely (especially if you are reckoning on only one turn), this gives you a volume of usable compost 2 by 2ft by 18in (61 by 61 by 46cm), which is not much more than a quarter of a ton. This is all right perhaps for a very small town garden but not much use to the serious vegetable gardener. In addition I think you will find a 3ft (0.9m) cube rather cramped to work in, for example when you are turning the heap. A 3½ft (1m) cube is a good size, giving you about half a ton of compost per heap , but I prefer to have a 4ft (1.2m) cube, partly because I find it easier to work in and partly because it will take a lot of material and there are times in the

garden when a lot is becoming available. At other times when material is short it is not necessary to fill the bin to the top. Provided you cover it with some sort of insulating material (for example, a double layer of old carpet) this will work very well. If you want more compost than this, I think it is better to have a double set of bins rather than one larger one. My garden heap is at present about 4 by 5ft (1.2 by 1.5m) on the ground and often rises initially to a height of 5ft (1.5m) or more, and I find this inconveniently large (see Plate 1). Throughout this chapter I am going to take a 4ft (1.2m) cube bin as the most satisfactory size, that is 4 by 4ft (1.2 by 1.2m) on the ground, and 4ft (1.2m) high, which will produce about one ton of compost per heap.

2. You are going to need two bins of this size – one in which you make the heap initially and the second into which you turn it. This assumes that you turn each heap once. We will discuss later what is involved if you want to turn it more than once. The most convenient way of arranging these bins is to place them side by side, forming a letter 'E'.

3. Made this way (with one turn) compost can be produced during the summer months (March to September) in about eight to ten weeks. During the winter it is more likely to take three to four months. I am going to assume that your double bin can produce four binfuls of compost a year, three during the summer months and one over the winter. This then amounts to a total of four tons of compost a year for a 4 by 4 by 4ft (1.2 by 1.2 by 1.2m) bin.

4. One ton of compost will provide sufficient compost for a depth of 1½in (4cm) over an area of 300 square ft (28m²).

From this you can now work out, firstly, how many bins you need and what size they should be and, secondly,

how large your total composting area needs to be and where best to position it.

Let us take as an example a standard 10-perch allotment, which is 30 by 90ft (9.1 by 27.4m), or a garden of roughly the same size. Quite a lot of this, however, will be taken up by paths, sheds and, of course, the compost area, so let us assume we have a cultivated area of about 2,000 square ft (186m²), that is about 45 by 45ft (13.7 by 13.7m), or 30 by 65ft (9.1 by 19.8m). Since 1 ton of compost will cover 300 square ft (28m²), it will take about 7 tons to cover 2,000 square ft (186m²).

As a double 4ft (1.2m) cube will produce 4 tons a year, you will need two double bins, producing 8 tons a year, which will give you a fair amount to spare. If you wish to have only one double bin, a 5 by 5 by 4½ft (1.5 by 1.5 by 1.4m) high bin will produce just over 2 tons per heap.

So how much space do you need altogether for your compost area and where do you put it? The other side of the coin is, how much choice do you have? How much space do you have to spare? For example, it is very convenient to leave plenty of room in front of your bins from which to work on them and plenty of room at the side to stack the various materials and tools you need. But if you are very short of space, some of this can be dispensed with. For example, you can abut the front of the heaps directly onto a path and work on the heaps from there and you can stack materials elsewhere in the garden and barrow them in when you need them.

Ideally you need 4 to 5ft (1.2 to 1.5m) at the front of your heaps for working on them, so in the case of a 4 by 4ft (1.2 by 1.2m) heap you need a total depth of 9ft (2.7m). Widthways it is convenient to have an extra distance roughly equal to the width of your

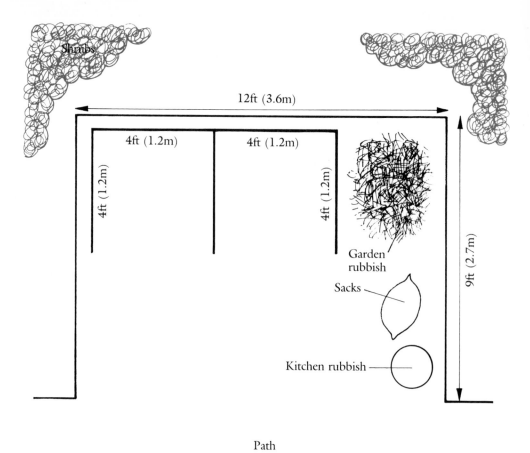

Shrubs

12ft (3.6m)

4ft (1.2m)   4ft (1.2m)

4ft (1.2m)

4ft (1.2m)

9ft (2.7m)

Garden
rubbish

Sacks

Kitchen rubbish

Path

SITING OF HEAP

heaps, that is, in this case, 4ft (1.2m), so you will need a total width for the area of 12ft (3.6m). This gives a total space of 9 by 12ft (2.7 by 3.6m). This, however, does not include any space you may need for a load of manure, which would have to be added on to this, unless you stored the manure elsewhere. Similarly for 5 by 5ft (1.5 by 1.5m) bins you will need an area of 10ft deep by 15ft (3 by 4.5m) wide.

Where should it be sited? Again, assuming you have the choice it should be:

- easily accessible by paths
- reasonably close to a water supply
- close to the kitchen (but not too close!)
- shielded from view

- reasonably level
- protected from sunshine and prevailing wind (this can be accomplished by using an area under shady trees that is not otherwise used as a growing area)
- have good drainage
- rest on soil (at a pinch it can rest on concrete provided it slopes slightly to provide drainage).

The general layout for a compost area is shown, left. A little later on, when we have learned a bit more about what is involved, we will give a more detailed and refined version of this layout (see page 36).

Some people may be a bit alarmed at these calculations and at the size of compost heap and compost area it appears they will need, and I would like at this point to offer some reassurance that will be repeated on various occasions throughout the book. I think that in writing about compost it is proper that I should be explaining and advocating what I have found to be the best way to make and use it, but to some extent this is a doctrine of perfection. As I said in the introduction, nature is on your side and, although it is good to be aware of perfection and to have it as your eventual goal, it is certainly possible to get by on less. For example, I have lived in London for a short time with a garden of 15 by 20ft (4.5 by 6), and we managed to make small amounts of compost in a corner underneath a lilac tree. And when I moved into my present house, I saw at once that the garden was in poor condition and would need a lot of compost. I did not have very suitable materials to make efficient bins, nor the time to collect them. I wanted to get on with making compost straight away rather than spend the time making compost bins, so

I knocked up a double bin with what came to hand (see Plate 1, page 32). These bins are inconveniently large and unsatisfactory in a number of ways (which I will come to in due course), but they have produced tons of excellent compost, and, although I intended them to be temporary, they are still in use two years later.

Composting is the corner-stone of organic gardening and even in a small garden the heap may produce many tons of valuable material each year, yet often the most well-organized gardeners seem to slide into slip-shod methods when it comes to composting. Having examined quite a number of garden compost heaps it is obvious that people take far less trouble and care with this operation than it demands. Even in financial terms a few pounds laid out at the start will soon garner a rich harvest.

The Compost Bin
So now we have our site and on it we erect a double bin. As pointed out above, it is as well in the first instance to make it either a temporary or a portable structure until you have made quite sure that the site you have selected is really right. We will now move on to the construction of your permanent bins.

Constructing the Bin
The material for making the bin must be strong, retain its shape, preferably be weatherproof and reasonably long-lasting. On all these counts wood, though expensive and getting more so every day, is ideal. On the other hand, one of the best heaps I have ever seen was in the angle between two sides of a brick-walled garden, the other two sides being corrugated iron.

Certainly when moving to a new house it is not necessary to wait until you have built yourself an executive-style compost bin before you start

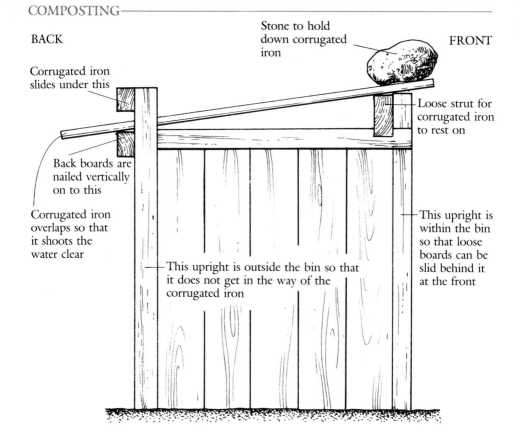

BACK

FRONT

Stone to hold
down corrugated
iron

Corrugated iron
slides under this

Loose strut for
corrugated iron
to rest on

Back boards are
nailed vertically
on to this

Corrugated iron
overlaps so that
it shoots the
water clear

This upright is
within the bin
so that loose
boards can be
slid behind it
at the front

This upright is outside the bin so that
it does not get in the way of the
corrugated iron

SIDE VIEW OF COMPOST BIN

making compost and indeed it would be
a mistake to do so before you have
tested out the site you've selected for a
season. In the short term a makeshift
heap composed of almost any materials
will serve to get you started.

I do not recommend wire netting or
empire fencing stuffed or lined with
newspaper. In principle this is a cheap
and simple method, but in practice the
wire gets out of shape and looks very
unsightly if one is not careful. It is also
difficult to fix on a stable roof.

It is worth keeping an eye on local
demolition sites or consulting the clas-
sified advertisements in the local paper
for suitable second-hand wood. So long

as the uprights are sound I see no
reason why one should not use planking
that has been discarded because of
woodworm and replace it as it breaks
up. Ideally the corner uprights should
be at least 5 feet (1.5m) long, preferably
of 4 by 2in (10 by 5cm), and the planks
one inch (2.5cm) thick.

A very good compost-bin material is
old doors. If you buy these in the
second-hand markets or through 'Articles for Sale' advertisements they are
quite expensive, but an enormous number of them just get thrown away. Most
council tips have (either legally or under
the counter) such articles for sale very
cheaply, but the best source of them is

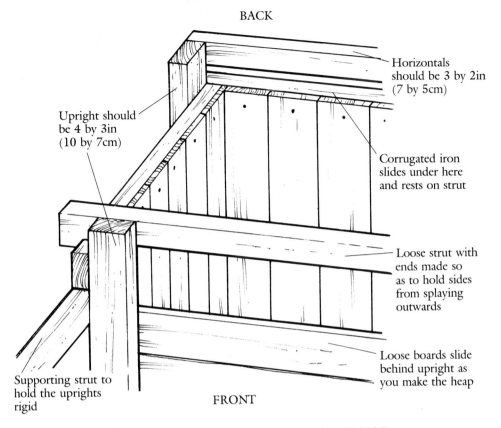

BACK

Upright should
be 4 by 3in
(10 by 7cm)

Horizontals
should be 3 by 2in
(7 by 5cm)

Corrugated iron
slides under here
and rests on strut

Loose strut with
ends made so
as to hold sides
from splaying
outwards

Loose boards slide
behind upright as
you make the heap

Supporting strut to
hold the uprights
rigid

FRONT

VIEW OF COMPOST BIN FROM THE TOP

builders' skips. Builders are, in my experience, always quite willing to give away any such materials that they don't want. You have to be quick off the mark, though, because anything of this sort left on a skip overnight is likely to disappear. When I came to build the bins shown in Plate 2 I acquired ten excellent doors within the space of ten days. Four of them I bought for £1.00 each and the other six were free!

The diagrams above show the basic method of construction.

For a really first-class job (once you have decided on a permanent site) you could concrete the corner posts into the ground; otherwise hammer them into

the ground to a depth of at least 15in (40cm). It is important that they should be creosoted or tarred where they will be underground, but otherwise left plain.

The fourth (removable) side often presents carpentry problems because the uprights are insufficiently stable and splay apart allowing the loose planks to fall out. It is therefore necessary to keep the uprights rigid, either by a loose strut which holds the side planks together, or by a strong, angled support.

Provided the heap is not too small and is not too exposed to sun, rain and prevailing winds, the fourth side can be left open, though it is preferable to close

Plate 1

When we moved to this house two years ago I could see at a glance that the garden was in urgent need of lots of compost and, as I had few materials available for constructing bins, and anyway no time for the work involved, I made do with what I could lay my hands on to make two *temporary* compost bins. Two years later the 'temporary' bins are still in use!

This picture shows the compost area as a whole. The heap in the right-hand bin is in the process of being turned into the left-hand bin. Just in front of the left-hand bin is a small pile of mature compost ready for use. In front of the right-hand bin is material accumulated for the next heap, including several bags of horse manure. The bags on the left contain wood ash. To the right of the bins is a turf heap that is 18 months old and ready for use. Apart from the area's general untidiness I am increasingly aware of these bins' defects, which I think are worth listing to help you with your own bins:

● They are too large for the average garden. You cannot reach the back from the front, which is inconvenient. They take too long to fill, so turnover is slow.

● They are under trees, which is fine, but they are so close that the ground beneath is a network of large roots. One of the trees is an ancient, very large yew, which in the autumn sheds layers of poisonous berries and needles which have to be removed.

● As I am right-handed, compost is made first in the right-hand bin and then turned into the left-hand one. But the right-hand one is by far the smaller of the two so that I have to pile it up inconveniently high and, even then, when turned it will only half-fill the left-hand one.

● The bins anyway are too high, especially the central division. When one is working towards the centre or back of the bin, one has to toss the compost over this 4½ foot (1.4 m) barrier into the next bin. This makes it far more laborious than it need be.

● The construction allows no convenient way of fixing a protective roof. In fact I have used carpet or underfelt or, as a last resort, plastic bags. These do provide some protection, but they are not wholly satisfactory as they don't drain the water away, so the compost tends to get too wet, in spite of some protection from the trees.

● Because it is 5 feet (1.5 m) long it is often necessary to work from the back of the heaps, but there is no convenient access to the back (on the left is the boundary fence, on the right of the bins is the turf heap, beyond that a pile of soil, then a pile of leafmould.)

● Although there is no shortage of space, there is no handy place to stack garden materials, bags of manure and so on for the next heap.

● I often find myself in need of compost and having to wait for a batch to mature; when it does I have to shift a large proportion of it to a separate pile to make room in the bin for the next batch.

● I have left to the last the fact that they are made of corrugated iron, because I have always found this reasonably satisfactory. It is true, however, it is not the ideal material – for one thing it gives very poor insulation to the heap.

In spite of these defects these two bins have produced many tons of excellent compost. The main problem is that the design faults make for a lot of unnecessary work.

Plate 1

Plate 2

Plate 2

My allotment compost area and bins are still incomplete. But if you compare them with the garden bins in Plate 1 you will see that most of the defects in the latter have been remedied except that to the right of my allotment bins is a wilderness of brambles, bracken and broom! You will see that here I have triple bins because the very poor soil is in need of very large quantities of organic matter so it is important for me to have a quick through-put. You can see in the *top* picture that I have started to build an allotment hut on the left of the bins. The idea is that they give each other mutual support, as the allotments are on high ground and open to strong winds. You will notice that the left-hand bin is higher than the others; the reason for this is that if I am short of time I do not need to shift the remains of the last batch but can leave them in their original bin and turn the next batch on top of them. I am not sure though whether this will prove a good idea over a longer time span and it presents a roofing problem that I have not quite come to grips with. The centre bin is a little too small because I unthinkingly measured it with a 2 foot 3 inch (0.69 m) door instead of with a 2 foot 6 inch (0.76 m) one. It is surprising what a difference that 3 inches (8 cm) seems to make! Note too that the top of the division to the left of the right-hand bin is removable so that you can take it out when you are turning the heap. This is shown in the picture *below,* where I am taking out the panel before turning the right-hand heap.

Doors are usually 6ft 6in (2m) long and either 2ft 3in (0.69m), 2ft 4in (0.72m), 2ft 6in (0.77m), or 2ft 9in (0.84m) wide. I think 2ft 6in (0.77m) is the best size and it is simpler to use doors that are all the same size. Make the division 3ft 9in (1.15m) from one end and 2ft 9in (0.84m) from the other.

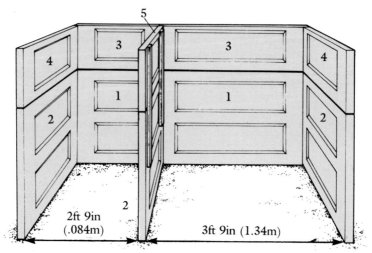

A DOUBLE BIN MADE FROM 8 SECOND-HAND DOORS
(Vertical posts, front pieces, etc not shown)

it, since, apart from anything else, this enables you to get more in your heap.

Two boxes should normally be built together in the form of an E, with each bin the same size. The bins must be covered, or coverable, most simply by corrugated iron which slides through the gap in the back and is held in place in the front by heavy weights. The roof slopes towards the back end so as to discharge water away from the heap and it is as well to have the ground sloping away from the heap where the water discharges so that water does not run back into it. For this reason it is advisable to have the corrugated iron long enough for there to be about a 12in (30cm) overhang at the back.

A possible alternative is an old carpet, (which, as it disintegrates, can later be incorporated into the heap) which you rest on the top of the heap when it is finished. This has the advantage of being a good insulator, but it is not very good at getting rid of the water and it is really better to use this as well as the corrugated iron roof rather than instead of it.

There are one or two refinements you can make to this basic design. Firstly, it is a good idea to have a space behind your bins where you can deposit the unwanted uncompostable fragments that always seem to find their way into compost material – wire, baler twine, assorted bits of plastic, wood, broken glass, etc. Every so often this area can be cleared and the rubbish disposed of in the dustbin.

Then if, as recommended, you are making a double E-shaped bin, it is an advantage to have one bin of the E about a third larger than the other. Compost material compacts down very considerably during the process of composting and so the bin you start it off in needs correspondingly more space than the bin you turn it into. If

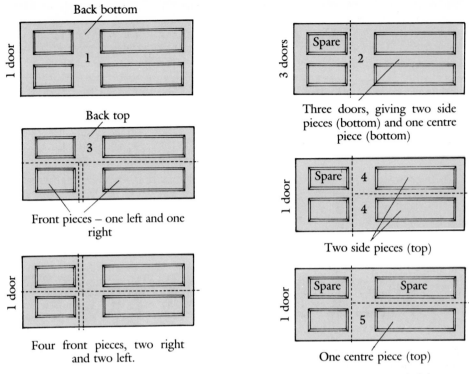

Back bottom

1 door

1

Back top

3

Front pieces – one left and one right

1 door

Four front pieces, two right and two left.

3 doors

Spare

2

Three doors, giving two side pieces (bottom) and one centre piece (bottom)

1 door

Spare

4

4

Two side pieces (top)

1 door

Spare | Spare

5

One centre piece (top)

----- Indicates saw cuts. Note that when cutting front pieces two saw cuts are needed, because the front must be a little shorter than the back to allow for the central division. It is important to cut this accurately so that the front pieces can slide between the sides of each bin.

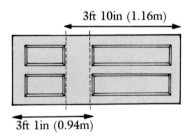

3ft 10in (1.16m)

3ft 1in (0.94m)

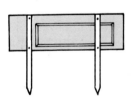

Cut the side pieces to whatever length you like. This length will of course determine the depth of your bin. The door above shows cuts in two places, giving lengths of 3ft 10in (1.16m), 3ft 5in

(1.04m) or 3ft 1 in (0.94m). It is easier to saw along the edges of panels, but if you do this you will have to fix a narrow batten on the loose end to prevent it falling apart.

Two 3ft (0.9m) battens fixed to the centre top (and also to the side tops if you wish) to hold them in place, so that they don't have to be fixed permanently but can be removed when necessary.

HOW TO CUT THE DOORS

not, your second bin will only be half full and space will be wasted.

Which bin should be the larger? That depends on whether you are right-handed or left-handed, for the natural action of shovelling is to swing across your body and not away from it (see Plate 3, bottom right). So, if you are right-handed, you will shovel from right to left and if left-handed from left to right. So for a right-handed person the right-hand bin should be the large one, and vice-versa. When I made my 'temporary' bin here, I inadvertently got this the wrong way round with the result that my right-hand bin is often filled to a height of 6ft (1.8m) or more, while the left-hand one is never more than half full (see Plate 4, top left). Throughout this book I am going to assume that you are right-handed and so the right-hand bin is shown as the larger. If you (or your principal compost-turner) are left-handed, this should be reversed.

Another point to note is shown in Plate 3, bottom right. So long as you are working near the mouth of the bin, you can shovel the compost round the outside when you are turning the heap, but as you move further in, this is awkward and the natural route is over the top of the dividing wall. As the picture shows, in this heap the wall is about 5ft (1.5m) high which means that you have quite a throw. For ease of action the dividing wall should not be more than 3ft (0.9m) high. It is therefore best to make a fixed division of about this height and, if you need to

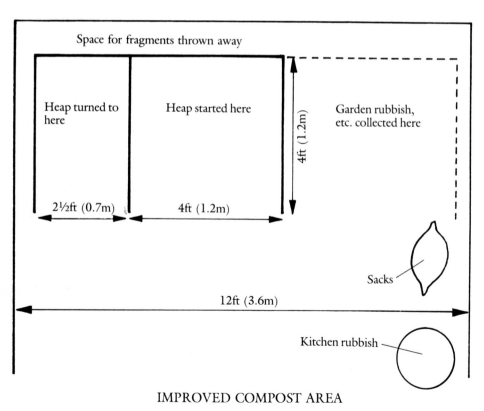

IMPROVED COMPOST AREA

increase the height, to do so with boards that are removable, so that when it comes to turning the heap these can be lifted out. This is shown in the diagram on page 35, part 5 and in Plate 2, bottom.

Lastly, you'll have noticed that in our composting area we have a space about the width of our bins in which to gather material together to make our first binful of composting material. To keep this in bounds and tidy, it is possible to make a third bin alongside your initial E. As this third bin would only be for gathering material and not for actually making compost it would not need to be of the same sturdy pattern as the proper bins. An amended diagram of your composting area is shown left.

Another type of container which is quite successful is made of straw bales (see page 58 for further details).

Ingredients

Now, what are we to use to fill our bins? First of all, of course, materials from our own gardens and kitchens, and, possibly if we can get it, those of our friends and neighbours. Secondly, it is astonishing how much organic matter it is possible to lay your hands on if you really try, even if you live in an urban area. The first thing to do is to provide yourself with a number of plastic bags. The one hundredweight fertilizer bag is very common and a useful size. In fact these bags litter the countryside and are becoming a serious disposal problem and anyone who has some will probably be willing to give you a few, for instance a local farmer, garden centre, greengrocer, provision merchant, etc. Electricity showrooms often have very large ones in which stoves are wrapped. However, if you cannot get hold of these it is possible to obtain waste disposal bags quite cheaply at your local store. If you then present these to your local grocer or greengrocer, there is a very good chance that he will allow you to fill them with his refuse. Street markets are also a good source of such material.

If you go to the seaside take a bag and collect seaweed; to the moors, peat. Ask your local brewery for hops or must; your local cidermaker for pomace; your local woollen mill for shoddy; your local maltster for kiln dust; your local seed merchant for spoiled seeds. Keep your eyes open for hessian sacks rotting in backyards, rotting leaves in ditches, wood ash from bonfires, lawn mowings dumped in the corner of the local park. Talk to the local parks superintendent and the road gangs. In the autumn collect leaves, in the summer grass mowings.

Every day huge quantities of organic matter, the precious end-product of millions of years of evolution, are wastefully disposed of in both town and country, and any keen and watchful enthusiast can reap the benefit. Do not worry if, to start with, you feel rather self-conscious and eccentric; people will not despise you for this activity, they will respect you; in due course your reputation will spread and small boys will travel miles to bring you a bag of horse-droppings or a couple of old birds-nests. Not only will you be collecting compost-material, you will be enriching your whole life, and other people's too.

Whatever you collect, keep it well sealed and tidy in its plastic bag until you are ready for it. Each time you have finished adding to the bag shake it down and tie it tightly with string, or fold the top over and hold it down firmly with a stone. Empty your kitchen waste into one of those large plastic dustbins with a lid. If it is very wet, as it often may be, mix some dry material with it, and cover it over with a piece of

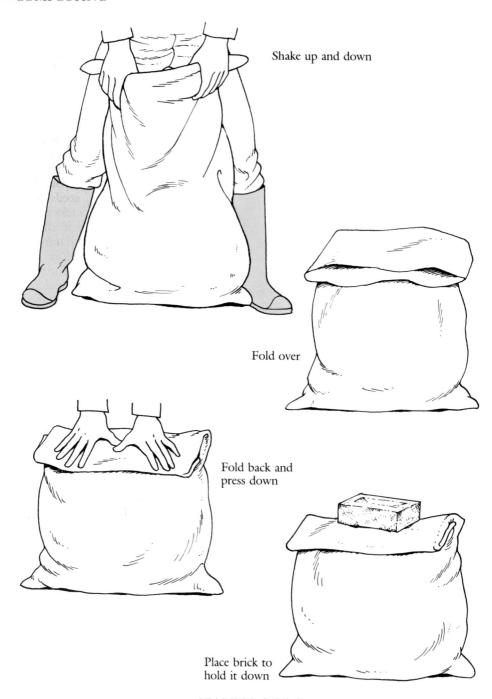

Shake up and down

Fold over

Fold back and
press down

Place brick to
hold it down

SEALING A BAG

plastic pressed down tight, as well as putting on the lid. If you do not have a spare dustbin, kitchen refuse can also be kept in a plastic bag, but press it down tightly so that no air can get in.

By now you will probably have tuned in to what we are doing. We are collecting all the ingredients for our compost heap, putting them in bags to seal them off so that no air can get to them and they cannot start decomposing aerobically, so that in due course when we have enough material gathered to make the heap in one fell swoop the material will be more or less fresh and not partially composted

already. It is possible to keep organic matter in its original state for a considerable time so long as you exclude air. For instance apple must, the residue of cider-making which is one of the most rapid and efficient compost ingredients there is will remain almost completely unchanged for at least twelve months. Even in the open, a large heap will form a strong dark impervious crust on the outside but will remain unchanged underneath. Once stirred or disturbed to allow the oxygen in, the heap will warm up and begin to decompose and turn dark within a couple of days. Similarly, hops will remain more or less unchanged for

Compost material in dustbin, plastic cover held down by bricks to keep it airtight

USING A DUSTBIN

several months in a sealed bag. The only change that may take place is for it to become a little more compressed, damp and sticky. When you use it you must shake it and fluff it a bit with your fork. Wet seaweed, however, if kept in bags for more than a week or so, will turn into a rather horrible, sticky, smelly mess.

Garden Rubbish

Meanwhile we are collecting our garden rubbish and this can be stacked in the space to the right of our first bin. Shake as much earth off the roots as possible for, although a compost heap benefits from some earth, there is, generally speaking, too much of this so you should avoid adding any extra. As far as composting is concerned, earth is an inert substance and tends to damp the process down. It can therefore seriously lower the temperature the heap will reach. This does not apply to the application of a 3 or 4in (8 or 10cm) outer layer of soil put on to protect the heap from the weather which will act as an insulation barrier and help keep the heat in. You should press all this material down and if possible cover it with a plastic sheet to discourage bacterial activity and to keep the area tidy. This process continues until you estimate that you have enough material to fill the first bin.

Building the Aerobic Heap

Now at last comes the day when you are ready to begin making your aerobic heap. You start by spreading a layer of garden rubbish in your first bin, follow this with kitchen waste, then add manure or other activator and any other organic material you have collected and continue with this until the heap is full. When you add the garden rubbish lay all the stalks and stems as far as possible lengthwise in the heap, that is from front to back. Try to toss everything in quite lightly so that there is plenty of air space, as it is on the presence of air (oxygen) that the process of aerobic fermentation depends.

Try to judge whether the mixture is too wet or too dry or just right. It should be damp enough to glisten without being actually wet. If it is too dry you must water it, and do not skimp the water. It is no good sprinkling water on it with a fine hose. It takes 12 gallons (54.5l) of water to dampen a bale of straw. On the other hand, do not forget that most green material is 80 to 90 per cent water and that this will be released when it decomposes. If you have a lot of dry material it is probably best to leave it out for a few days in the rain before you use it. If the material is too wet, mix in some dry matter as you make the heap.

Once you have used up all your materials and the heap is finished, cover it with sacks or an old carpet or a 2in (5cm) layer of soil – anything to keep the heat in. Put on the corrugated iron roof and the job is done. This is shown diagramatically on pages 44-45.

Dry Materials

I said above, mix in dry materials, and it is worth looking at what suitable materials there may be available.

Bonfire ash should be gathered dry and stacked away in sacks.

Wool shoddy, if you can get it, is wonderfully water-absorbent, though it has to be broken up and fluffed out before using it.

Remains of old potting compost etc, should be dried out and bagged up for such an occasion as this.

Peat is of course the ideal material if you

As far as possible stalks laid lengthwise

Strut

Loose boards

FILLING THE FIRST BIN

can afford it – that is, the light-coloured very dry sphagnum peats like Irish Shamrock peat, not the dark sedge peat from Somerset, which normally has a very high water content itself.

Do not use newspaper, it will go soggy.

You can use sawdust in very small quantities, but it decomposes slowly and too much will certainly hold the heap back. In fact apart from this special use I don't generally recommend using sawdust in the compost heap.

What to Avoid

What to avoid? Very little, except that this is the stage when you should consult the list on page 17 showing proportions of carbon and nitrogen. If you have not got the proportions approximately right your heap will not heat up, and you will need to take a

plastic bag and a shovel to Trafalgar Square (pigeon droppings have one of the highest nitrogen contents of any manure) or attend a few meetings of the local hunt or visit your local garden centre with a credit card in your pocket. The shortage of nitrogen is one of the key limiting factors in compost-making and is referred to again later in this chapter under 'activators'.

What else to avoid? Well, how confident are you, from experience, of creating a heap that will heat up to around 150°F (65°C)? And how willing are you to turn your heap at least once so that the outside edges which did not heat up are turned to the inside? If the answer to either of these questions is 'no' then you should avoid putting in the more malevolent perennials. Do not worry so much about docks and dandelions and the like, they can be recovered fairly easily and it is worth trying to compost them down by feeding them through several cycles. It is the more insidious and pervasive weeds, ground elder, convolvulus, celandine, which have very little to contribute to the compost heap or the soil and for which there seems no alternative to a total, if undeserved, annihilation on the bonfire. You should also be chary of including diseased material of any sort since, however well you turn your heap there is always a chance that some portion of it will not heat up. Don't include crops suffering from club root as there is some suspicion that the organisms concerned survive the heat of the best-made compost heap. Take care if you use a lot of bracken (see page 88).

Avoid also leaves from the following trees: conifers, yew, holly and laurel; fish or meat residues from the kitchen; anything not organic (such as plastic, metal and man-made fibres); hard or woody materials such as brassica stalks, raspberry canes, hedge clippings (unless they are very soft and chopped small). Brassica stalks, however, can be used in the trench for runner or climbing beans, if mixed with a layer of manure. When I read about this (in an HDRA newsletter) I was a bit sceptical, but I tried it and, to my surprise, when I lifted the bean plants at the end of the season I found the stalks and manure had decomposed into a beautifully fine homogenous layer of compost.

The Next Stage

So now your heap is made and it lies enigmatically smouldering beneath its canopy of carpets and corrugated iron. What is going on within its mysterious depths? Nervously you regard it and try to uncover its secrets. What imperial splendour, what heights of thermophilic ecstacy are being scaled, what depths of bacterial squalor are being plumbed?

So far there is no Gibbon to trace the intricate webs of this history, for even the scientists are baffled by the incredible variety and complexity of it. But you do have a rough yardstick of whether all is well, and that is the temperature. You do not need a thermometer for this but a simple iron pipe 2 or 3ft (1 metre) long. You push this in towards the centre of the heap, leave it for a couple of minutes and then withdraw it. If it is too hot to hold comfortably by its business end, then your temperature is above the 120°F (49°C) range and all is going well. After about a week you will probably notice that your pipe is coming out a little less hot than before and this is a sign that your heap is beginning to turn anaerobic and the slow decline has begun.

Turning the heap

Now you have a choice before you: to turn or not to turn? The situation of your heap at this stage is this. The centre of it should be pretty well free of weed seeds and of all but the largest and most resistant perennial roots; that is to say, these things will still be there, partially decomposed perhaps, but no longer capable of germination. It will be by no means decomposed, but a start will have been made – that is assuming, of course, that your heap has maintained its temperature over most of the previous week. The outside of the heap, however, will have changed very little and will be full of weeds and weed seeds. If left now it will probably take another two to three months (in the summer), before the centre is well broken down. At that stage you can chop off the outer 6in (15cm) all the way round and transfer them to the next heap; the rest can be forked out, removing any large lumps together with any assorted, uncompostable objects that always seem to find their way in via

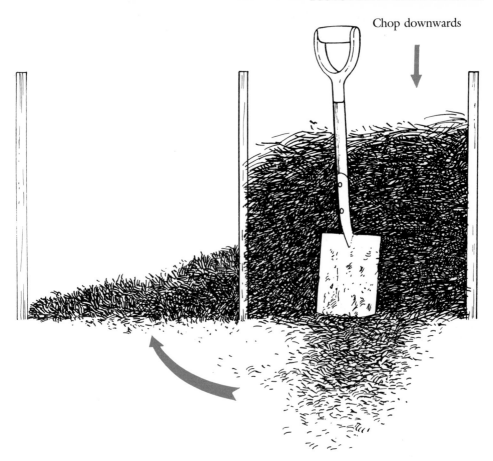

Chop downwards

BREAK UP AND FORK INTO NEW HEAP ALONGSIDE

the kitchen wastes such as milk bottle tops, toothpaste tubes and plastic bags. It should then be used as soon as possible.

Alternatively you can greatly improve both the speed of action and the quality of the end product by turning. The essential implement for this is a fairly heavy spade with its end sharpened on a carborundum stone or grindstone to razor sharpness. This is used on a guillotine principle to slice off the outer end of your heap into roughly 1in (2.5cm) sections. You can do this quite rapidly, like a French chef chopping up

leeks, so long as there is not too much tough matter (especially tough grass) in it. That is why the stalks and other hard materials were laid as nearly lengthwise as possible – by this process the whole of your garden material is chopped up into the sort of size that will decompose readily.

When you have chopped a fair pile, toss it as lightly as possible into the second bin and return to your slicing. Again, keep a careful eye open for uncompostable fragments, simply throwing them out to the back of the bin. Watch for moisture content and, if

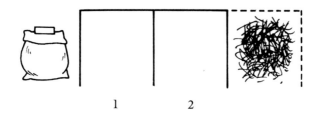

Accumulate garden rubbish.
Accumulate other materials in plastic bags, well sealed.

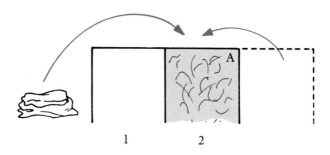

As soon as you have enough material, use it to build heap in bin 2.

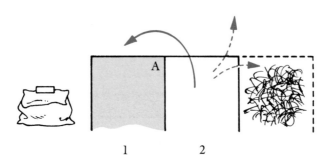

After one or two weeks, turn heap A into bin 1, removing any uncompostable fragments, and recycling compostable rough material back to the garden rubbish heap. If there is any compost left in bin 1 from a previous heap, that must be used or stacked elsewhere. Continue to accumulate materials for next heap.

SCHEME FOR MIXED AEROBIC/ANAEROBIC HEAP

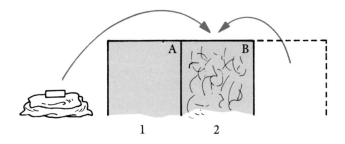

As soon as you have enough material repeat the process, building heap B in bin 2.

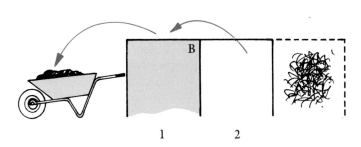

As soon as compost in bin 1 (remains of heap A) is used up (or perhaps stored elsewhere), turn heap B into bin 1. Now bin 2 is empty and ready for heap C as soon as you have accumulated a further supply of material.

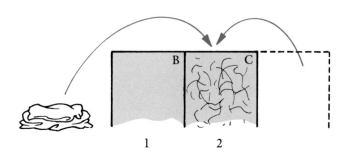

This process can continue to operate indefinitely.

Using two bins to produce monthly one ton of compost
that has been composted for six weeks and turned twice.

Make heap A in bin 2.

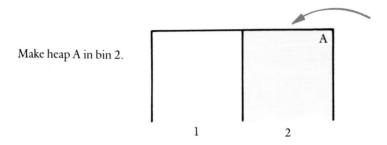

Two weeks later.
Turn heap A into bin 1
and leave bin 2 empty.

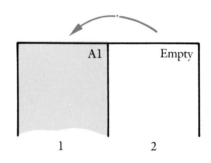

Two weeks later.
Turn heap A back into
bin 2 and make heap B in
bin 1.

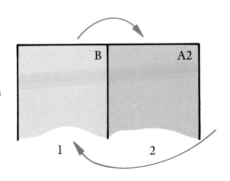

TURNING TWICE USING TWO BINS

Two weeks later.
Use heap A.
Turn heap B into bin 2
and leave bin 1 empty.

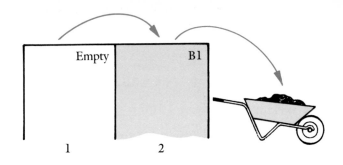

Two weeks later.
Turn heap B back into
bin 1 and make heap C in
bin 2.

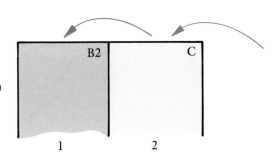

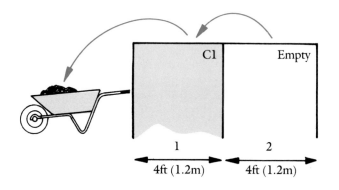

Two weeks later.
Use heap B.
Turn heap C into bin 1
and leave bin 2 empty.

Repeat the procedure
for the next batch of
compost.

necessary, correct it. Watch out also for heavy lumps or other material that look as if they are going to be slow to break down and return them to your garden rubbish heap for recycling. It is likely that both at the top and the sides and front of your heap the majority of the material will be best returned for further composting.

Continue with this process until you have emptied your first bin and filled your second one. The second bin should now once more become aerobic and heat up again. As the temperature declines this will mature and if all has gone well it should become ready for use within a further three to four weeks. Meanwhile your first bin is now empty and ready for starting a new batch as soon as you have sufficient materials, unless you decide to turn your first heap a second time as soon as its temperature begins to drop. If you do this you will be approaching the situation of a fully aerobic heap.

It is sometimes claimed that one turn is sufficient to create sterilized compost provided that you turn the outside of the original heap into the centre of the turned heap. I am doubtful whether this is so. It may possibly be true for large heaps where the proportion of outer unsterilized material is small in comparison to the size of the heap, but for the ordinary garden heap the amount of material in the centre that heats up sufficiently to become sterilized is too small. Let us take the example of the 4ft (1.2m) heap. At a rough guess the temperature in the outer 6in (15cm) will reach a level insufficient to sterilize it, no matter how well the heap is made and insulated. This means that the material in the centre, which is just about half the heap (31½ cubic ft (0.89m³) out of 64 cubic ft (1.81m³), to be precise) may, if the heap was well made, be sterilized and the outside half

(32½ cubic ft (0.91m³)) will not. So when you come to turn it, the outside half has to be placed exactly in the centre of the new heap, and the inside 6in (15cm) round it. This may be possible theoretically, but in practice there is no hope of placing the unsterilized half so accurately in the centre that some part of it does not project out towards the sides where it is likely to remain still unsterilized.

I think a 6 by 6 by 6ft (1.8 by 1.8 by 1.8m) heap is the smallest in which you can feel sure of turning the outer 6in (15cm) layer of the initial heap securely into the centre of the turned heap so that it heats up enough to be sterilized.

A 6 by 6 by 6ft (1.8 by 1.8 by 1.8m) heap will produce nearly 4 tons of compost and I think that this is inconveniently large for anyone to handle without mechanical aids, and is, anyway, inappropriate for the average garden. My experience is that for a 4ft (1.2m) heap two turns are the minimum needed for sterilization and three turns are preferable if you want to be on the safe side (that is, if you wish to include perennial roots or material that may be diseased or if you are going to use the compost for potting or if you are concerned that it should be entirely weed-free).

The diagrams on the previous two pages show how to turn each batch twice using only two bins. Three observations are worth making. You start each new batch alternately in bin 1 and bin 2, so bin 2 will no longer be automatically the starting heap and there is no advantage in making it larger than bin 1. Also, one of your turns will be from left to right, which you will find slightly more awkward than the other way round. And thirdly, one bin remains empty for two weeks and this wastes space and holds up the steady flow of compost through the system.

When turning each heap twice, it is better to make three adjacent bins, so that there is a steady flow from right to left. This could produce a new batch of compost ready for use every two weeks, whereas the two-bin method only produces a batch every four weeks. Three bins will not take up a lot more room than the two-bin method because both the left-hand bins can be considerably smaller than the full-size starting bin (see page 51 and Plate 2).

I should add that these are somewhat idealized diagrams where you turn your heaps regularly every two weeks and compost each heap for exactly six weeks. In practice it will not be like this: you are unlikely to achieve such mechanical perfection even if you have a regular supply of compost ready to hand and a willing composter on the standby to turn it. What it does mean is that, if at any time you are suddenly in need of a lot of compost, you have, with three bins of these sizes, the ability to produce a regular supply of one ton every fortnight.

It may seem that all this talk about insulation and maintaining the temperature is irrelevant, since the turning process must cool it down almost to nothing. This is true, but as a matter of experience the fact is that the enormous boost the heap receives from its renewed supply of oxygen will bring the temperature right up again within two or three hours after turning.

Activators

Compost activators fall into two main classes: material containing a high proportion of nitrogen, and products whose mode of action is a little obscure but which appear to work as bacterial stimulators or inocula.

The need for the first has already been made clear. The optimum conditions for aerobic bacteria require a mixture of materials in which the proportion of carbon to nitrogen (the C/N ratio) is about 30:1. But the C/N ratio of most garden weeds averages 60-70:1 and to bring this closer to the required ratio we must add materials with a much lower C/N ratio, in other words with a much higher proportion of nitrogen. As such materials are rather hard to come by they have been put in a special category and called activators.

Natural activators are manure, especially chicken manure, urine, pomace (cider residue), hops, comfrey, or any of the materials in the list on page 17 with two or more crosses under nitrogen. Chemical activators are sulphate of ammonia, or any of the nitrogenous fertilizers. Most of the proprietary activators you buy in shops consist principally of chemical nitrogen fertilizer in one form or another. Generally speaking activators of this type do not have any advantage over an ordinary chemical nitrogen fertilizer and the decision which to buy is a matter of comparing costs.

The convinced organic gardener will not use a chemical activator, but many uncommitted people argue that it is better to have a chemical activator than no activator at all. This is a debatable point and I do not think that at present there is any convincing evidence comparing the quality of compost made with organic activators against that made with chemical activators.

A Natural Activator

For some people the issue does not arise because there is one very good organic activator available to everyone who is willing to take a little trouble, and that is what is politely known as *night soil*. Urine is one of the very best sources of organic nitrogen there is, and is freely available to everyone in quantity. The only problem, apart from the embarrassment that some people experience in the operation, is how to apply it without waterlogging your heap.

The best method is to have a large plastic bin, in which you place a layer of dry soil, peat, sawdust or other dry material (not newspaper). Add the daily dose of urine, and continue to add dry material so that it does not become waterlogged. As a second best you can add it to your anaerobic pile of garden weeds, again with an admixture of dry materials, and cover it over tightly with plastic. Inevitably by this method a certain amount will seep away and be lost and the plastic bin method is undoubtedly better. There is no reason why you should not use the same bin as for your kitchen rubbish: make sure though that it has a piece of plastic held down tightly as a seal.

If you use this method you should not need to bother with any other activators, but whatever you do it is important that you are aware of the problem of nitrogen and of the need to take it seriously.

The Chinese have also used human faeces to maintain the fertility of their soil for a period of 4,000 years. Most Westerners regard the suggestion that they should think of following suit with considerable squeamishness, although they don't seem to worry about the fact that their drinking water has been recycled, on average, 11 times. See my comments on Chinese composting and on 'human manure' on page 22.

Food, water, air, warmth: who can decide which is the most important to life? It is impossible to say since they are all essential. It is more a matter of which of them is in short supply and difficult to obtain. Water is free; air is free but has to be made available by turning; if not its absence will act as a limiting factor. Warmth is taken care of by insulation. Food is the other limiting factor, the necessity to have a balanced diet, and the primary importance of the balance between carbon and nitrogen.

As for the second class of activator, it is very hard to give advice. It has always seemed to me a sort of miracle that this huge and variegated microbial army should assemble and go into action spontaneously and naturally, without any of the elaborate planning that preceded D-Day. The exact details are not known because of the difficulty researchers have had in isolating and studying the individual facets of this multifarious operation. The mere fact of isolating an organism is liable to change its behaviour and even structure in ways that are very hard to determine.

What is evident, though, is that there are very large numbers of different organisms involved in the process and that the ones that prevail depend very much on the particular ingredients of the heap. These emerge in the very rapid 'survival of the fittest' operation which develops, and there is no evidence either theoretical or in practice to suggest that any external stimulus is necessary or beneficial.

What is sometimes claimed is that supplementing the natural population of organisms will enable the whole process to develop more rapidly and efficiently; the suggestion being that there is an initial time-lag, during which the bacteria sort themselves out, which can be eliminated by providing the right organisms with some sort of boost. But several studies (notably at the University of California, the main centre for research into composting) have failed to establish that such a time lag exists. All the evidence seems to confirm that if the right conditions are present decomposition will take place without external aid, and that if the right conditions are absent no amount of activators of this sort will make good the deficiency.

Using three bins to produce every two weeks one ton of compost that has been composted for six weeks with two turns. (Note that this system only takes up one foot more space than the two bin system.)

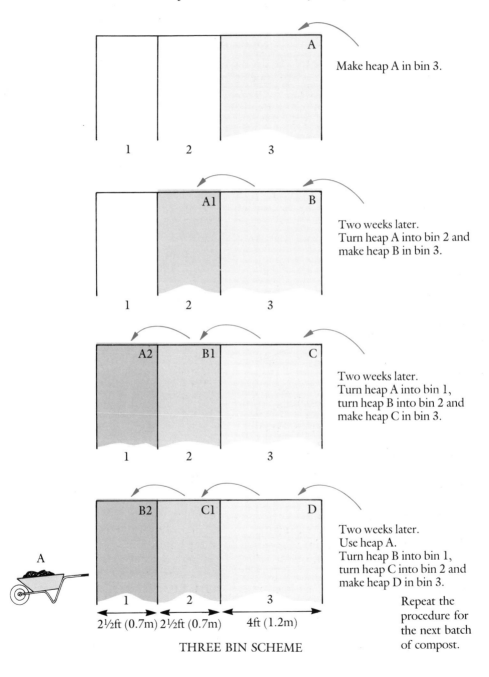

Make heap A in bin 3.

Two weeks later.
Turn heap A into bin 2 and make heap B in bin 3.

Two weeks later.
Turn heap A into bin 1, turn heap B into bin 2 and make heap C in bin 3.

Two weeks later.
Use heap A.
Turn heap B into bin 1, turn heap C into bin 2 and make heap D in bin 3.

Repeat the procedure for the next batch of compost.

2½ft (0.7m) 2½ft (0.7m)   4ft (1.2m)

THREE BIN SCHEME

Every two weeks (15 days) you produce one ton of compost that has been composted for three weeks (20 days) and turned three times. If you are a weekend gardener you could vary this by making the interval seven days instead of five and still produce about 15 tons of compost a year. Again, I think it would be better to have four bins if you propose to turn the heap three times, and this would enable you to produce an almost continuous supply of compost, provided you have sufficient raw materials and enough time and energy to do the turning. I must confess I haven't and so have never tried it, but I am of the opinion that it isn't possible to guarantee fully sterilized compost with less than three turns.

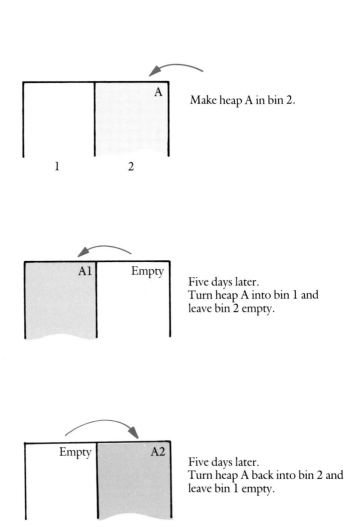

Make heap A in bin 2.

Five days later.
Turn heap A into bin 1 and leave bin 2 empty.

Five days later.
Turn heap A back into bin 2 and leave bin 1 empty.

SCHEME FOR FULLY AEROBIC HEAP USING ONLY TWO BINS

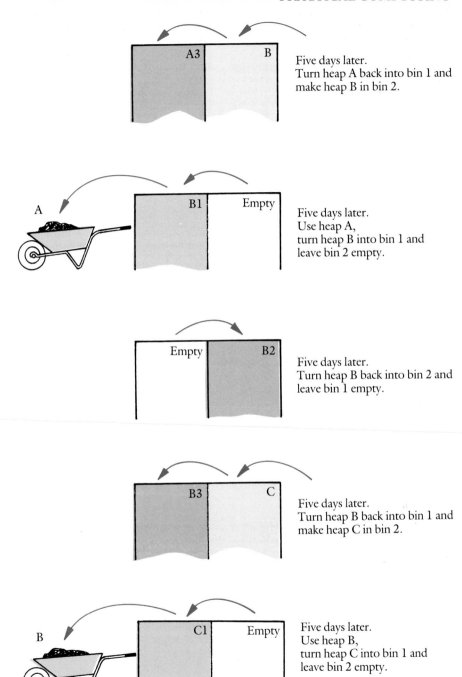

Five days later.
Turn heap A back into bin 1 and
make heap B in bin 2.

Five days later.
Use heap A,
turn heap B into bin 1 and
leave bin 2 empty.

Five days later.
Turn heap B back into bin 2 and
leave bin 1 empty.

Five days later.
Turn heap B back into bin 1 and
make heap C in bin 2.

Five days later.
Use heap B,
turn heap C into bin 1 and
leave bin 2 empty.

Repeat the procedure for the
next batch of compost.

However, it must be conceded that many observant gardeners have used one or other of these activators for years and are convinced of their benefit. At no stage is scientific research infallible and there is still a vast amount to be

Horse Manure Heap A well-made manure heap like this one (the only defect being that it has not been made under cover – see page 116) with frequent large additions of good strawy manure will remain aerated and therefore decay aerobically at a good temperature for far longer than a mixed garden heap. The centre of it should produce good sterilized composted manure without turning. If I wanted this I would be delving further into the middle, but what I need is an activator for my compost heap so I am taking fresh manure from the side.

With the huge increase in the number of horses in this country and the decline in demand for horse manure by mushroom growers (many of whom are now using chemical activators instead of manure) there should be no lack of good free manure for anyone who is prepared to search it out, and of course to fetch it.

learnt about how compost heaps work and how best to make them. I would suggest that as an insurance that is both trouble-free and cost-free it is a good idea to incorporate a proportion of compost from previous heaps into the new heap, say about ten per cent, which works out at about twenty good spade-fuls for an average-sized heap, spread as evenly as possible throughout the centre of the new heap. It has already been suggested that the partially composted front and top of the old heap should be carried forward to the new one, and this I should think should serve the purpose.

Manure

Manure, having a comparatively high nitrogen content is the commonest activator of the first sort (that is, the sort that provides nitrogen) and probably the best. It must however be fresh, as 'well-rotted' manure will already have been digested by bacteria and become composted, and will have lost its value as an activator. To keep manure in a fresh condition so that it may be used over the season, and also to prevent it smelling and causing a nuisance to over-sensitive neighbours, it must be tightly sealed in bags or kept tightly under a plastic sheet. This will slow down decomposition to a minimum and prevent loss of nitrogen.

Manure is usually bought mixed with straw. There should not be too much straw or all its value as an activator will be used up in decomposing the straw and there will be no surplus for your needs. An undue excess of straw will tend to retard a compost heap because of its very high cellulose content and the difficulty of breaking it down. On the other hand, if there is a shortage of straw, manure is rather difficult to handle as it forms into sizeable lumps that are completely anaerobic and will take a long time to break down. In this case, it needs to be thoroughly forked and fluffed around so that it does not lie in heavy wet lumps.

The above remarks apply only to manure as an activator. Of course if you lay in a load of manure for use direct on the garden it may be 'well-rotted' and this will save you the trouble of composting it down yourself.

Lime

It is not normally necessary or especially desirable to add lime to a compost heap at any stage. If you live in an area of acute acidity and feel that there is a need for some neutralizer, the use of calcified seaweed is preferable to lime.

It is, however, a good idea to measure the acidity of your finished product, and very simple kits are now available for doing this. Acidity is measured by a number, known as the pH value, which will usually lie between 5 and 8. Most plants grow best in a soil with a pH of between 6.4 and 6.8, and if your compost has a value very much below this it is advisable to apply a sufficient quantity of lime or calcified seaweed to bring the pH up to 6.5. This is likely to happen if decomposition has been mainly anaerobic, and it can serve as an indication that for the best results an aerobic heap should be aimed at next time. Lime should not be applied to fresh manure as this will lead to a loss of nitrogen in the form of ammonia. The same will apply to a compost heap before it has decomposed unless you know from experience that it is excessively acid. In a normal aerobic heap the acidity will vary somewhat throughout the cycle, but will end up about correct, that is, at about 6.5. For use of lime as a soil conditioner, see page 94.

Woodash

Woodash is valuable because it is a source of potash, one of the principal nutrients required by growing plants. It is often applied directly where it is known to be especially valuable, for instance to beans, potatoes, tomatoes and gooseberries. Otherwise it is better to incorporate it into the compost heap rather than apply it directly for reasons explained on page 93.

As already mentioned woodash can also be valuable when the compost ingredients have become too wet. If this is liable to be a problem for you, you should collect it when it is dry and store it in waterproof sacks until the need for it arises.

Granite Dust

Granite Dust is sometimes recommended, especially in America, either as an additive to the compost heap or as an organic fertilizer or leaf spray. Its exact function or value has not been clearly explained, but it possibly results from the fact that some granites contain a proportion of potash-felspar which could become converted in the compost heap by either microbial or chemical action into forms which make it available as a plant food.

Dolomite

Dolomite is magnesian limestone and contains up to 50% magnesium carbonate as well as calcium. It can be used instead of lime on land that is deficient in magnesium. It is an accepted fertilizer that is approved by organic purists.

Another way of overcoming magnesium deficiency is by spraying plants or the soil with a diluted solution of Epsom salts as they contain magnesium sulphate. I have seen this recommended by organic gardeners though strictly speaking, of course, magnesium sulphate is a chemical product and is no more organic than ammonium sulphate.

Phosphate

As well as nitrogen and potash, and to a much lesser extent magnesium, phosphate is the other principle nutrient required by plants. It is not often in short supply but bad soil conditions, especially too acid a soil, can lock it up and make it unavailable. However, if you employ some of the green manuring techniques mentioned later some extra phosphate may be advisable. This will be dealt with in the chapter on green manure. A similar technique can be used for phosphate as was suggested for potash, that is, a chemical fertilizer such as superphosphate can be added to the compost heap which will turn it into an organic form which will become available slowly as it is needed. This would definitely not be approved of by the dedicated organic grower and unless you have good reason to believe that your soil has a serious long-term phosphate deficiency it is not a course to be recommended.

Animal-Free Compost

There are a number of people who on ethical, religious or horticultural grounds prefer to use an animal-free compost. It is worth pointing out two things: one is that the natural process upon which compost-making is based involves a variable mixture of both animal and vegetable matter; the second is that no compost is strictly speaking animal-free since every ounce of it contains many millions of bacteria, to say nothing of the detritus of larger animals, worm-casts, bird droppings, etc. However, these are not conclusive arguments against this point of view, and the whole question of animal-free organic fertilizers is one which demands the attention of those who wish to increase our area of arable land at the expense of mixed farming, and who are also opposed to chemical fertilizers.

For the garden composter, an animal-free compost poses a serious problem of how to provide an adequate supply of nitrogen, because although such sources as hop manure, pomace and seaweed do exist they are not readily available or cheap. Grass mowings and other greenery contain a fair percentage of nitrogen but as this is usually calculated on a dry weight basis and as green plants are roughly ninety per cent water this does not amount to much in practice.

The best plan would be to devote a small area of the garden to a permanent patch of comfrey, and to grow as many legumes as possible (peas, beans, lupins, etc.) as these have the ability to fix nitrogen from the atmosphere and are consequently far the best nitrogenous source amongst common garden plants; and in addition to adopt a fairly ambitious scheme of green-manuring: this will be dealt with in Chapter 4.

Drainage

If the end product of all your labours is wet and sticky and has a sickly brackish odour of putrefaction, one possible cause is inadequate drainage, a common source of bad composting. It may be that you have positioned your heap in a bad place and nothing can be done about it except to move it. Usually however matters can be improved by raising the heap above ground level. This can be done by leaving the bottom six inches of compost, though of course if this is also wet and sticky, as it almost certainly will be, it cannot be left in this state. This is an occasion when sawdust can be used. The compost should be forked fairly deeply, a large quantity of dry sawdust mixed and turned with it and the whole stamped down again. An inch layer of sawdust can then be spread on top before beginning the new heap, partly to act as a damp-course and partly

as a warning against going too deep when you are taking out the compost.

Leaves

Small quantities of leaves may be used in the heap, but should be mixed in with the other ingredients rather than spread together in layers. If you can get hold of large quantities of leaves these should be made into a separate heap. However, this is not quite so straight-forward an operation as it sounds as they tend to take up an enormous amount of room and to blow all over the place and you find you need four arms each four feet long – it is rather the same sort of problem as stowing a spinnaker in a force eight gale.

Leaves can be contained in the following way: take a length of 4ft (1.25m), 2in (5cm) wire netting and build a fence by weaving 5ft (1.5m) stakes through the mesh and knocking them a foot into the ground in such a way as to create a container 4ft (1.25m) wide: you will need 20ft (6m) of wire netting for a 6 by 4ft (1.75 by1.25m) heap and 24ft (7.25m) for an 8 by 4ft (2.5 by 1.25m) heap. Pile your leaves into this container, watering them if they are dry (you will need a large quantity of water) and then stamp them down. When this is done, lay a length of netting 4ft (1.25m) wide along the top and hold it down with stones.

After a year the heap will have partially decayed and formed itself into hard dense layers, and it should be removed by the same guillotine process as described for the compost heap. It can then be used direct on the soil in appropriate places, or incorporated into the next compost heap where it will have much the same beneficial effect as the addition of peat.

On its own leafmould is excellent for putting into the seed bed, since it increases the humus content and hence

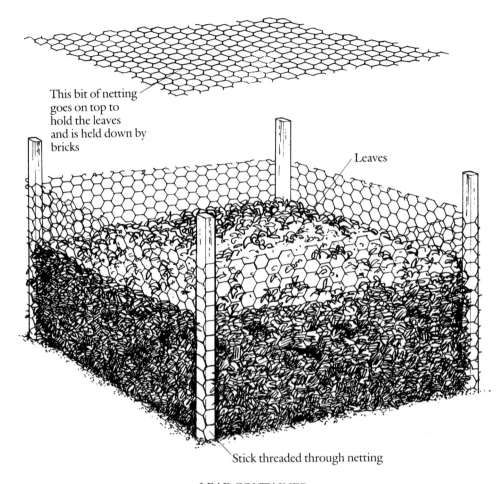

This bit of netting goes on top to hold the leaves and is held down by bricks

Leaves

Stick threaded through netting

LEAF CONTAINER

the quality of the soil without unduly increasing the nutrient content. It also tends to be rather acid, so it is useful for correcting a soil that is over alkaline, but this has to be watched in a soil that already tends to acidity.

Leafmould can be such a valuable free bonus for your garden that it is worth going to a little trouble to collect some of the thousands of tons that are wasted every year. This is where a few of those very large plastic bags from electricity showrooms would come in useful.

Straw Bales

One system sometimes advocated is to build the sides of the compost bin with straw bales which after one or two seasons are incorporated into the compost and replaced by further bales. This is an attractive idea for country dwellers with large gardens and large compost heaps. Two cautions need to be uttered: one is that the bales may contain a wealth of weed seeds some of which will certainly spread into the compost. The second is that when they do come to decompose they will need the addition of a very large quantity of nitrogenous matter because of their high ratio of carbon to nitrogen. There is also a danger that selective weed killers were used when the straw was grown. Some of these can remain in the plant for a considerable time and continue to be effective. Many glasshouse crops were lost from this cause when the system of growing on straw bales became popular in the sixties. Ideally therefore only straw grown without weed killer should be used. Unfortunately our planet is now so contaminated by pollutants of all kinds, insecticides, herbicides, radio-active waste, chemical over-fertilization, lead from petrol fumes, industrial pollution, to mention but a few, that attempts to create a healthy soil are almost as problematical as attempts to maintain a healthy atmosphere.

Rough Heap

At various times it has been suggested that such things as brassica stalks, some perennial weeds and wiry grass etc., should not be put on your compost heap, and it is worth considering for a moment what can be done with these. The simplest answer is to burn them and add the ash to the heap. On the other hand compost, like human beings, benefits from a certain amount of roughage, and there may be danger that our compost lacks this constituent.

Brassica stalks being mostly cellulose, may be of uncertain value, but there is no doubt about the richness in a dandelion root or a dock; they have delved deep into the earth in search of sustenance and as a result are a mine of mineral wealth. If there is a spell of fine weather and you have the space there is something to be said for spreading the roots out to wilt and dry but this is unlikely to guarantee that they will not

grow again; it takes a great deal of drying to sterilize the roots of some persistent perennials. A better plan is to compost them, once again laying them fore and aft so they can be sliced into small sections, ready to incorporate later into your fast heaps.

This rough heap will of course decompose anaerobically, so perennial roots will not be destroyed. However, it is surprising how much it does break down, provided you keep the weeds cut down and prevented from growing all over the place.

This rough heap is an annual affair, in fact it can easily be left to run on for two years, so it needs to be considerably larger than your normal heaps; being anaerobic it is not essential that it is boxed in, provided you take care not to allow it to spread everywhere.

When you do decide to use it, wait for an opportunity when you have a good supply of fresh manure or other activator. Then guillotine it down as described on page 43 and place it carefully away from the edges of your aerobic heap.

Soil

It is often recommended that soil should be added to the compost heap. Generally speaking there is enough soil in the roots of garden weeds, and in many cases too much. Soil is not necessary in a compost heap, as the example of a manure heap, consisting only of dung and straw, demonstrates. Excessive soil acts as a damper, just as it does in a house fire, or as graphite does in a nuclear reactor. When it can be useful, again as in a bonfire, is as an outer casing to act as an insulator. A three inch layer of soil, or of inverted turves, laid neatly on the top of a completed heap, will have this effect. Soil can be used to a much larger extent in an anaerobic heap, for example, of

Rough Compost Heap This picture shows a rough heap built somewhat on the lines of the Chinese 'earth heap'. It is 10 feet by 4½ feet by 4 feet (3 by 1.4 by 1.2 m) high and will produce 6 to 8 tons of composted soil, which will cover around 2000 square feet (186 m²) to a depth of 1 to 1¼ inches (2.5 to 3 cm). Unlike the Chinese, I allow weeds and/or green manure plants to grow on the top and sides, and I use these in my ordinary compost heaps. In this picture I have just sliced the weeds off the sides, using a sickle. The top still has a very weedy growth of fenugreek.

inverted turves (see also Chinese 'earth compost', page 22).

Failures

Suppose you have done the very best you can, read all the books, understood them, followed all the instructions, and still your heap produces only a black slimy mess, or a tangle of uncomposted roots?

The main causes of failure have already been mentioned, but here is a summary of them:

1. Too wet or too dry. Is your heap properly protected from the weather? Is it waterlogged from below?
2. Wrong admixture, especially no activator and therefore not enough nitrogen. Also too much hard or woody material.
3. Too much soil, especially perhaps too much heavy clay.
4. Loss of heat. Bin made of corrugated iron, or with big gaps.
5. Material not chopped up properly and/or not mixed up properly, for example layers of grass mowings.

The best course for you to take is to remake or turn the heap, making good the defects as you do so in the ways already described.

CHAPTER 3
HOW TO USE COMPOST

Before we actually come to use the compost we should take a good look at it and also at the garden soil. The sort of bacterial bonanza already described as taking place in the compost heap is only an intensification of what is happening everywhere. A teaspoonful of ordinary garden soil is said to contain over 1,000,000,000 organisms. These organisms are all beavering away, going through their spiral of conversion and recycling which is effectively never-ending. Whatever the condition of the soil, there are micro-organisms that can adapt to it. Even if the soil is sterilized it will be recolonized eventually; if it is sprayed with poison new organisms will evolve that are adapted to survival. Such action will of course harm and perhaps even partially destroy it temporarily, but only some major cataclysm – a new ice age or nuclear explosion – will destroy life altogether for a long period.

The degree of activity will depend, as in the compost heap, upon the conditions – food, water, air, temperature. In an active soil the nutrients (food) will be continually altering their structure and composition as a result of which there will be a steady stream of nutrients changing into forms that are available as plant food. At the same time the bacteria will as far as possible be maintaining their own environment, the soil, in a condition that suits them, that is open, aerobic, damp, warm – the very same conditions that suit plant growth; in fact there is a happy balance between the needs of the plant and the needs of the bacteria.

It is, I think, important to realize that there is no guarantee, or likelihood, that this balance is especially favourable to the human race or indeed that we have any necessary part in it. On the contrary, it seems evident that with our present numbers and mode of life we completely upset the natural cycle of birth and death, growth and decay. It is because of this imbalance that with heavy-handed arrogance we intrude our own demands and conditions, asserting the right to totally transform the environment to our own advantage.

What we as compost gardeners are attempting to do is to carry out this transformation in a way that does not too brashly offend against the creative balance that exists. The application of compost is designed, quite simply, to improve the conditions in which a wide range of soil bacteria can operate so that both the physical condition of the soil is satisfactory, and a steady supply of nutrients becomes available as plant food as it is needed.

To this end, the first thing to do is to take a critical look at the compost we have produced. Is it really the black, crumbly, homogeneous, sweet-smelling material we were led to expect? Or is it cold, grey, glue-like, lumpy and full of inexplicable bits of wire and plastic and long gleaming white roots? If so, these objects must of course be picked or forked out. Now, look again: is it shot through with uncomposted fragments, strawy material, roots, and so on?

If the latter, let us consider what will happen when you mix it into the topsoil: the uncomposted straw represents a surplus of undigested carbon, which is one of the basic foods for bacterial growth. The other two critical needs for bacterial growth are oxygen, which will certainly be readily available in the top soil just after it has been disturbed, and nitrogen, which is probably in short supply or else the straw would already have decomposed. So the bacteria with their natural tendency towards maximum growth, will seek for nitrogen in every nook and cranny of their environment. All the nitrogen therefore which would in the natural course of events have been or become available for plants will instead be recycled back into bacterial growth. It will remain in the soil, and will eventually reach that stage in the cycle where it again becomes available to plants, but for the moment it will not because if there is competition between plants and bacteria for scarce resources, the bacteria will win every time; in this event your plants will suffer from 'nitrogen starvation' and will not grow properly but be chlorotic and stunted. If your compost is as described you have two options: either to sieve it carefully, using a one inch mesh sieve, and recompost the residue; or else to put it on in the autumn and use it to grow a green manure crop, so that it is broken down and ready for use in the spring. The first is probably the better alternative in most cases.

Taking a Soil Profile

The next thing to do is to take a look at your soil, and I would recommend that you take a soil profile. To do this it is usually recommended that you dig a hole three feet deep and to do this it is necessary to make the size at the top at least three feet square, so as to enable you to step it down to reach the required depth.

For our purpose a hole 18in (46cm) square at the top and 18in (46cm) deep would be sufficient. One of the downward faces should be sliced clean and even so that it can be examined. In a fairly typical soil the top few inches will be brown and well matted with roots and other fibrous material. Below that will be a layer of between four and eight inches which is also brown and still has a fibrous texture. These two together make up the top soil which is the most important layer from the point of view of plant growth. Below this there will be another layer which is much lighter and which may very well be rather greyish in colour. This is the subsoil. Below this again you may come to a soil which is quite highly coloured, particularly yellow or red or red-brown. This difference in colour between the two layers is caused by the washing down of iron compounds by rain, and suggests that very probably plant foods and lime are being washed down as well.

Examining the Top Soil

Now take a further look at the top soil. How deep is it? How dark is it? How much organic matter does it contain? What sort of texture does it have? What about the subsoil and the parent soil below? Both of these are important partly because they give a clear indication of the basis of the top soil; partly because of their effect on it – for example as regards drainage; and partly of course because plant roots will be growing into them: even many annuals have a very wide and deep root system: the roots of carrots for instance will penetrate seven feet or more. Is it sandy,

Plate 3

Top This compost heap was made in early May and the photograph was taken about four weeks later. Originally it was 5 feet (1.5m) high but has now sunk to 3½ feet (1m). As it sank I stacked garden refuse for the next heap on top of it, to save space and to provide insulation and protection from the weather. When I turn the heap I remove this first.

Below left This picture shows the slicing action used when turning the heap. The spade I am using is very sharp but not quite heavy enough. In the same way that a small, light saw, however sharp, is harder work than a heavy one, which will do the work for you, a heavy spade is much better than a light one. It is worth keeping a small cement trowel handy for scraping the blade. Heavy spades are hard to come by, but for those who holiday on the continent, I recently bought a very good, heavy, long-handled spade, made in Germany, in a small local ironmonger in France that was not very expensive.

Below right I am moving the sliced material into the next bin. When the pile is big enough to be able to pick up a good forkfull I use a fork, but when it is small it is easier to use a shovel. Note that the action is right to left (I am right-handed). Note also the effort involved in tossing it over the high dividing barrier. This is wasted energy.

Plate 4 (overleaf)

Top left This picture shows the heap once it has been turned. The left-hand bin is only half full due to the bad proportions I noted earlier. People often complain about how much time and effort is involved in making compost. The amount of compost I have made here is about 2½ tons (5 feet by 4½ feet by 3½ feet (1.5 by 1.3 by 1.0 m)) and it took me 1 hour, 50 minutes to turn it (and I am a pensioner, not overly strong, and have a serious heart condition!) With a well-designed bin, a younger, stronger person should very easily be able to halve this time.

Top right A month later and the compost is ready for use.

Below The garden in late July. When the mid-season strawberries are over, I cut the plants down to ground level immediately after harvesting and then spread a 1 inch (2.5 cm) layer of compost on the strawberry bed. As you can see, this encourages new growth wonderfully during the rest of the summer and builds up the plants' strength for healthy crop production next year.

Plate 3

Plate 4

Plate 5

Plate 6

Plate 5

Top left Part of my allotment, in May, in a generally weedy condition – and even the weeds are not growing very vigorously! What it does not show is that lurking underground is a whole network of bracken roots all ready to spring into action in June! I took over the allotment on 1 April and if I had had to clear the whole of it, it would have taken all my time and I would never have got to sow and care for any crops. Mulching a part of it, as shown in Plates 6, 7 and 8, enabled me to cultivate the whole of it, even if some of the resulting harvest have not been quite up to exhibition standard!

Bottom left The allotment in early July, showing at the front, from left to right: young, newly layered strawberries, cardoons, interplanted with salad bowl lettuce, celeriac, two rows of asparagus, parsnips (very small because the first two sowings failed to germinate), scorzonera, salsify and, to the far right, the brassica patch. Behind, on the left, are broad beans (behind these the earth compost heap), courgettes, a row of peas already harvested, runner beans, pinched out for an early crop, and, adjacent to these, climbing French beans for a crop later on. Beyond that is the compost area in the making, and in the background the advancing tide of bracken. The soil in the foreground, as you can see, is extremely poor and an alternative plan could have been to have limited myself to a few key crops and devoted all my energies to making the remaining soil more fertile rather than to have tried to grow edible crops on it straight away.

Plate 6

I marked out the whole area with sticks to indicate the positions for plants, and in early June I cut the weeds right down and dug a hole at each position, which you can see *top left*, that I filled with a mixture of clean soil and compost, and stamped this down firmly (*top right*). I then laid the carpet roughly in position, and left it until the time came to transplant.

The picture *below left* shows the seedbed in my garden. Transplants are grown in narrow slits between glass (rescued from some cast-off louvre windows) to protect the plants against cabbage-root fly. It is common practice to protect plants after transplanting them, but by then it is often too late as cabbage-root flies are active in May and June. Originally the glass was tight up against the plants on each side but has been moved during lifting. The rows are watered copiously before lifting, and *below right* you can see the transplant ready for planting out. Note that the ball of damp soil remains intact with no roots disturbed or showing.

(See also the notes on page 96.)

DIGGING A THREE FOOT SOIL PROFILE

silty or clayey? Take a small knob of reasonably moist soil and rub it between your fingers. If it feels gritty and does not dirty the fingers, and cannot be moulded into a cohesive ball, then it is a sandy soil. If it is gritty but can be formed into a ball and does not dirty the fingers then it is a sandy loam. If it is not gritty, but sticky and becomes polished when you roll it between your fingers, then it is a clay. If it feels smooth and silky but does not become polished, then it is a silt. If it is none of the above, forms into a cohesive ball and dirties the fingers then it is a loam.

A sandy soil is greedy for humus and uses it up very quickly. A rather rough, heavy compost is best for it, preferably made from cow or pig manure. You must also pay attention to conserving moisture by mulching, providing shelter and, in very hot weather, shade and by disturbing the surface as little as possible. Disturbing the surface will aerate the soil that is disturbed and this will increase the bacterial activity and the bacteria will mineralize the organic material in the soil, breaking it down into water-soluble salts that will be leached out of the soil by rain-water. Thus, disturbing the surface of light, sandy soil will tend to decrease its organic content and its nutrient content. This is why I prefer a no-digging technique for sandy soil. You should in any case watch the supply of nutrients, for example a shortage of potash indicated by brown spot on broad beans, or of nitrogen, indicated by stunted growth and pale sickly leaves. Sandy soil is also very likely to be an acid one and to need very frequent liming (or treatment with calcified seaweed).

If your soil is clay, the addition of lime will help to create a surface tilth for sowing. There is usually no serious shortage of humus or nutrients, and composting should aim at creating a more open soil texture and a more workable soil. Deep-rooting green manure plants will be helpful in improving drainage.

Silt is one of the most difficult soils to work and the need to add large amounts of humus makes the composting and green manuring system outlined in the next chapter especially applicable.

Using Your Compost

We will now proceed on the assumption that you have a fair idea of the type and quality of your soil, and that by one means or another you have achieved a reasonable heap of good quality compost, and now the question is how best to use it.

First of all there is no avoiding one indisputable fact: compost is like money, it is far harder to make it than it is to spend it – and there is never enough, not nearly enough. Therefore every bucket of compost must be used with thrift and care. The important underlying principle is that it should be used when and where plants are growing, that is at root level in the vicinity of plants at the time of maximum growth. So do not spread it all over the garden indiscriminately; do not use it as a mulch except in special circumstances, and do not put it on in the autumn to overwinter. Use it as soon as you are able to, and put it where it will have the most immediate effect. There is a myth that whereas chemical fertilizers, being water soluble, very quickly leach out of the soil, organic fertilizers and compost somehow last for ever. This is not exactly true. If compost is put on the soil in the spring its effect will have mainly dispersed by the autumn – not entirely because there will be some residual improvement in the quality of the top soil, but it will not be very noticeable.

The truth is that if compost is spread wholesale over or in the soil where it is not being used fairly immediately its effects will be largely wasted. Similarly if it is heaped up in a pile in the open waiting for the time when it is needed, some of its potency and good effect will be lost.

Luckily compost is mainly produced during the warm months from April to September, and this is precisely the time when it is most needed. Overleaf is a list of suggestions of where best to use it for different months, though this will of course depend upon the latitude and the weather conditions. An extra cold year in the north of Scotland could be a month behind an extra warm one in St Ives.

Plants That Must Have a Rich Soil and Plenty of Compost

Strawberries, raspberries, blackcurrants, cauliflowers, sprouts, sprouting broccoli, celery, celeriac, runner beans, main-

March/April	Seed bed, new potatoes, early peas, onions.
May	Greenhouse, asparagus mulch, globe artichoke mulch, strawberries, soft fruit, raspberries.
June	Runner beans, maincrop peas, planting out brassicas.
July	Planting out brassicas, celery, celeriac, leeks.
August	Planting out brassicas.
September	Planting out seakale and spinach beet.
October November	Broad beans, hardy peas.

crop peas, asparagus, globe artichokes, onions.

Plants That Will Produce a Reasonable Crop on Less Good Soil

Lettuces, summer turnip, summer beetroot, spinach, swedes, seakale and spinach beet, Jerusalem artichoke, leeks, savoy cabbages, kale, broad beans.

It should be understood that there are very few, if any, vegetables that will not do better on a well-composted soil; the above are ones which will produce some sort of worthwhile crop on soil of only medium quality.

Plants Which Definitely Dislike Fresh Manure or Rough Compost

Carrots, beetroot, parsnips, salsify, scorzonera. Spring cabbage is best planted out in the autumn in a soil that is not too rich in nutrients, otherwise it grows too strongly and will be damaged by frost. It will need a boost of nitrogen in the spring, though, and this can be best given by spraying the leaves with an organic fertilizer.

With this information it should be fairly easy to know how best to allocate limited supplies of compost, and the following notes mainly amplify the obvious.

For plants and seeds that are normally trenched, a one or two inch layer of compost is put in the bottom of the trench and the seeds planted in it. When planting leeks or potatoes by the dibber method a small handful of compost is put into each hole, and the plant set on top of it. Salsify and scorzonera can be sown by making a hole with a crowbar, filling with a mixture of sifted mature compost and fine soil which is watered and firmly compacted, and sowing two or three seeds in the centre. Long parsnips are best sown that way too if your soil is in the least bit heavy, and even maincrop carrots if you want a good crop in a heavy soil.

In poor soil small seeds can be sown as follows: make a small trench about two inches wide and one and a half inches deep. Water thoroughly if the weather is dry; fill with damp compost, tread down firmly and level off with the back of a rake, and sow the seed in this.

When transplanting brassicas or other plants (except spring cabbage) make a larger hole than necessary and

SOWING SALSIFY, SCORZONERA OR PARSNIPS IN
A CLAYEY OR STONY SOIL

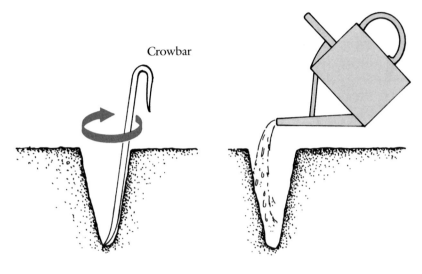

Crowbar

Make a
conical hole
10-15in (25-38cm)
deep

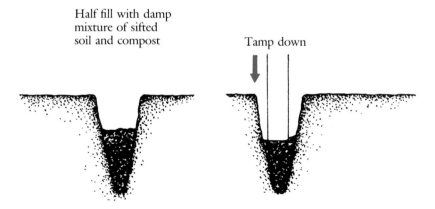

Half fill with damp
mixture of sifted
soil and compost

Tamp down

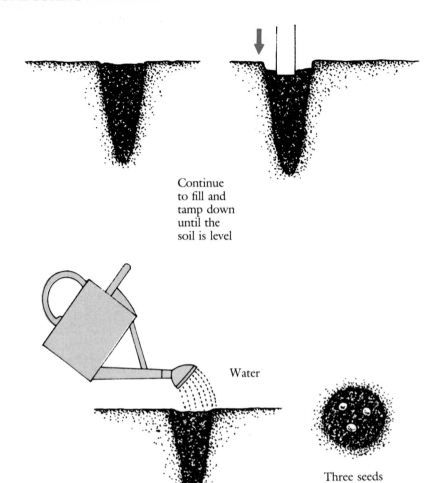

Continue
to fill and
tamp down
until the
soil is level

Water

Three seeds

 Three
seedlings

Thin to
one

plant in compost. Personally, I always plant mine using a method very similar to that shown on page 72-73 for planting shrubs and I think this definitely pays off.

Seed Bed
It is often said you should not put too much compost on your seed bed because this will result in a growth of seedlings that is too rapid and sappy. This might be true if you put on too much very rich compost, but this is not very likely – there is far greater danger of too little.

The conditions necessary for good seed germination are warmth; air (oxygen); and moisture.

The need for oxygen means that the soil must be open, that is, it must have a good tilth; the need for moisture means that although open it must not dry out, that is, it must have a good content of organic matter; and the need for warmth requires it to be light in texture and dark in colour.

All this points to a soil with a high proportion of organic matter, and the seed bed is the one place where you must be prepared to spread compost over the whole area. In addition if you have been using peat for storing roots, or for forcing chicory, or for blanching celery, or in potting compost, it is on

the seed bed that it should end up. It is difficult to say how much compost you should use, because it rather depends upon how you manage your seed bed in other respects, in particular how much topsoil you take off on the roots when you are transplanting. In general you should aim to spread at least one inch depth of compost or peat every year, that is, at a rate of about one barrowload for a bed eight by ten feet (2.5 by 3m).

Planting Fruit Trees, Shrubs etc.
The main aim when planting is to induce a prolific root growth well below the surface so that the plants grow rapidly as soon as the soil warms up in the spring and so that they do not dry out in the warm spells of May and June. Many shrubs (for example raspberries and roses) have a tendency to surface rooting with a consequent danger of drying out during hot spells; it is necessary therefore to maintain a good rooting system well below the surface to guard against this, which is why it is so important to incorporate compost *beneath* the roots at planting time. Trees and shrubs cost quite a lot of money nowadays and will continue to give you service for many years. A little extra care at planting will affect them permanently so it is really worth taking that extra

Wrong: plant potato and then fill with compost

Right: put in a handful of compost then plant potato in it

PLANTING POTATOES BY DIBBER METHOD

care. The following method should be observed very carefully.

Preparation of the Soil

It is essential that the soil should be very firm at planting time; therefore any preparation should be carried out at *least* four weeks in advance to allow the soil to settle. It is very bad to dig out a lot of deep-rooted perennial weeds one day, and plant trees in the same soil the next. But if this does happen the only thing to do is to ram and stamp the soil down as much as you can though you should of course exercise moderation if your soil is, for example, heavy clay. If your soil is too acid, counteract this with calcified seaweed in preference to lime.

Arrival of Plants

If you cannot plant immediately lay them out and cover roots with several layers of damp sacks or damp soil. On no account must the roots be allowed to dry out. This is very important. If they are container grown, leave them in their containers till planting time, placing them in a sheltered position out of wind and sun. Remember to keep them moist by watering.

Preparing for Planting

Trim roots (in the case of young shrubs to about twelve inches long), removing any that are damaged. Shorten top growth. Mark the bed with sticks to make quite sure where you want to plant.

Planting

You will need a one-gallon bucket of water per plant (two if the weather or soil are dry) and a bucket of compost, (two if the soil is poor). If you have any wool shoddy, horse hair or bristle, this is a very good place to use it for it will continue to decompose, slowly releasing nitrogen over several years. It is very important that it is thoroughly wetted, especially in the case of shoddy.

1. Dig hole one full spit deep with spade. Put the top soil on one side and the sub-soil in a barrow to take away.

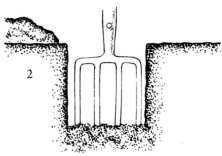

2. Loosen soil for another spit with fork.

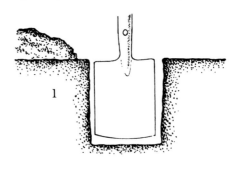

3. Incorporate half your compost into the second spit, mixing it with the soil. Ram this mixture down *very firmly*.
4. Pour on half the water.
5. Mix the other half of the compost with the top soil from the hole.

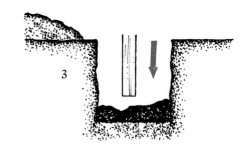

6. Make a conical mound at the correct depth (this is unnecessary if plants are container grown.) Unless otherwise instructed this should be at the same depth as the plant was grown in the nursery, indicated by the soil mark around the stem.

7. Place tree or shrub on mound, spreading roots neatly all round it. If it is a windy site lean the plant slightly *away* from the wind. If the plant is container grown make sure it has been thoroughly watered before planting so that when the container is removed the soil or compost will remain attached to the roots. (Note that occasionally containers may consist of peat pots which should not be removed but should be *thoroughly* soaked in water.)

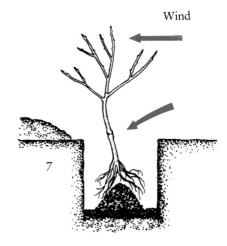

Wind

8. Add about 6in (15cm) of soil/ compost mixture. Rock the plant gently back and forth so that the soil gets right round the hair roots, using your fingers to push it through the roots. Once again ram the soil down firmly.

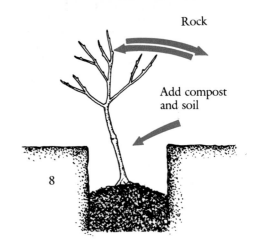

Rock

Add compost and soil

8

9. Go on adding the soil/compost mixture firming down as you go, to about 1in (2cm) from the top.
10. Pour on the other half of the water.

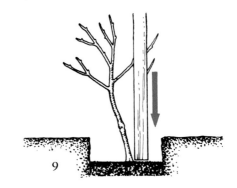

9

11. Spread the remainder of the compost/soil mixture loosely on the surface.

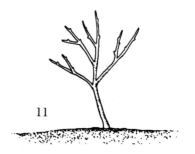

11

For normal soils, the amount of water suggested is the absolute minimum even in damp conditions or rainy weather. In dry conditions more will be essential. The only possible exception to this is if you live in an area of badly drained heavy clay. This problem is dealt with below.

Firm planting is absolutely essential. It is no good just treading the soil firm at the end as this will leave loose soil underneath just where it matters: the soil must be firmed as you go. If your soil is very clayey and sets like concrete you must add more compost to counteract this but you must still make sure it is firm.

Dealing With Clay

There is one situation where the method described above will not work and that is if your land is a low-lying heavy clay that will not drain, for example much of the Thames Basin. What happens here is simply that the rainwater runs into your nice well-composted, well-drained soil and fills up your hole where it remains indefinitely, waterlogging your plant's roots. There is not really much you can do about this short of digging a simply enormous hole, but even this is likely to fill up eventually during the rainy season. The best thing to do is to dig a large deep hole and stack the clay by the side of it. Where there is bad drainage there is very likely to be a hard pan beneath the surface, which may be 2-3ft (0.6-0.9m) down. If there is, it is important for the hole to penetrate this

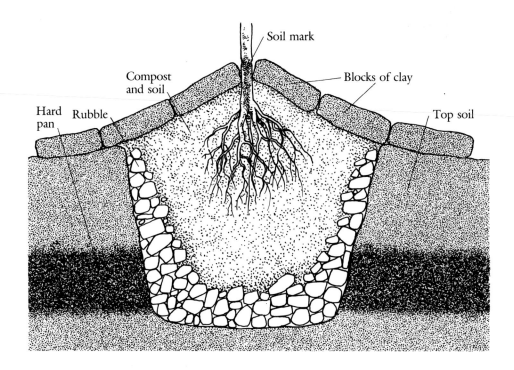

Soil mark

Compost and soil

Blocks of clay

Hard pan   Rubble

Top soil

FIRM PLANTING

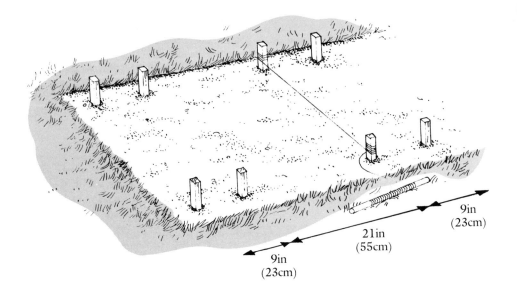

9in
(23cm)

21in
(55cm)

9in
(23cm)

so that water can drain beneath the pan. Fill the bottom and sides of the hole with drainage material, for example mortar rubble or crushed and broken bricks. Plant your tree in a mixture of soil and compost in the normal way, but set the soil mark a little above the level of the soil, building up the compost to this level. Finish off with four inch slabs of clay as shown on page 75.

What you are doing, in effect, is to protect your roots and the soil they are growing in by roofing them in with clay, allowing only quite a small area for the necessary moisture to drain in. All this involves quite a lot of time and trouble, but the only alternatives are to avoid growing trees and shrubs in this sort of area, take a chance that you may lose the plant and your time be wasted, or go to the even greater trouble and expense of installing a system of field drains.

The Fixed Row System
The general guidance given in this chapter should enable any gardener to adapt his gardening practice to compost methods. This book is not intended to be a gardening manual but because the problem so often arises that there is not enough compost to go round I am going to describe now a system of organising the garden that is intended to make the maximum use of what compost there is.

The basis of this system is that the same area should be used year after year for growing crops that are heavy feeders and that this area should receive the main bulk of the compost, whereas the intervening areas need not be composted to the same extent or even at all, and will be used for the light feeders. Here, what was said earlier should be repeated: there are very few plants that do not prefer a well-composted soil, but there are some which will produce a reasonable or at any rate usable crop in soil of only medium quality, whereas there are others that it is just not worth growing unless you have high quality soil.

The basis of this system is that the garden, or a portion of it, is marked out permanently in strips 9in (23cm) wide and 21in (58cm) apart. All your compost, or the greater part of it, is applied within the strips, and the great majority of the heavy feeders are grown in double, single or triple rows within the same strips. The intervening 21in is used to interplant the light feeders, and to grow green manure crops if you adopt the green manuring procedures outlined in the next chapter. Certain permanent crops of course exist outside this system, for instance asparagus or soft fruit. Others also seem better outside it, for example, Jerusalem artichokes, because of their growing habits. Apart from that it is possible to adopt any distribution of crops or any rotation that suits you.

The first thing to do is to mark out your bed with permanent markers. These should be straight strong stakes about 20in long which should be hammered a foot into the ground and should remain there permanently. The bed should be measured out accurately and stakes should be placed at each end of the rows. When you are sowing or planting you should always use a line and this should be wound round or aligned to the stakes. Occasionally the stakes can get loose or get kicked out or broken, and then they should be replaced at once.

A typical rotation over a cycle of three years would be as shown below.

In the spring of Year 4 start again with a similar rotation, but now with the benefits of three years of concentrated composting.

The advantages of this scheme are obvious, but there are of course some disadvantages, which do not seem to me to amount to very much, but which should I think be mentioned:

1. Adhering to it does require a considerable amount of discipline and planning. The position of the rows

Year 1	Year 2	Year 3
Spring Plant maincrop potatoes in trenches with 2in (5cm) of compost	*Summer* Harvest beans and hoe off at surface level leaving roots to rot	*Spring* Lift brassicas. Level off and plant parsnips, scorzonera, salsify, etc
Autumn Harvest potatoes and follow with triple row of broad beans in trenches with another 2in (5cm) of compost	Plant brassicas, preferably sprouts or broccoli (now called 'winter cauliflower') or sprouting broccoli	*Spring/Summer* Intersow with spring onions, cos lettuce, spinach, beet, carrot
	Summer/Autumn Inter-plant with crops of brassicas: either transplant kohl rabi, summer cabbage, or sow catch crop of turnips or radish	

TYPICAL ROTATION

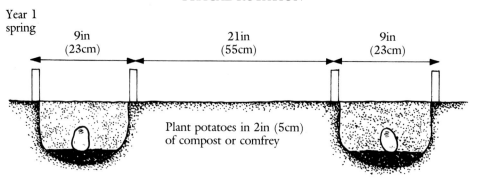

Year 1
spring

9in
(23cm)

21in
(55cm)

9in
(23cm)

Plant potatoes in 2in (5cm)
of compost or comfrey

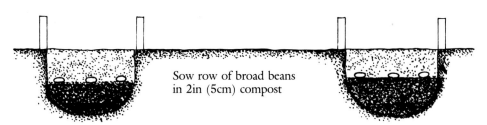

Year 1
autumn

Sow row of broad beans
in 2in (5cm) compost

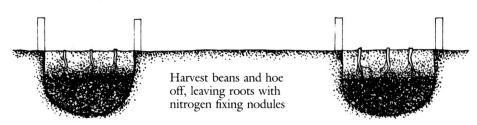

Year 2
summer

Harvest beans and hoe
off, leaving roots with
nitrogen fixing nodules

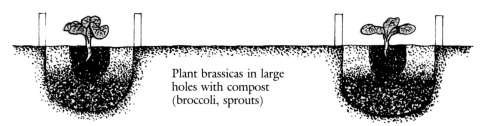

Year 2
summer

Plant brassicas in large
holes with compost
(broccoli, sprouts)

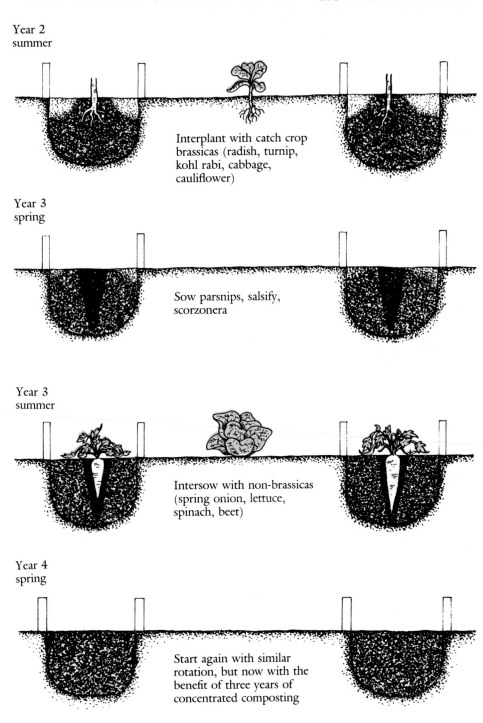

Year 2
summer

Interplant with catch crop
brassicas (radish, turnip,
kohl rabi, cabbage,
cauliflower)

Year 3
spring

Sow parsnips, salsify,
scorzonera

Year 3
summer

Intersow with non-brassicas
(spring onion, lettuce,
spinach, beet)

Year 4
spring

Start again with similar
rotation, but now with the
benefit of three years of
concentrated composting

must be carefully marked and adhered to. Intercropping must be carefully planned and must take advantage of the period when main crops are not too large or too vulnerable.

2. The distance between rows is geared to the crop requiring the greatest distance, that is 2½ft (0.76m). But the fact is that whatever the gardening books may say, the distance between rows is arbitrary anyway and is as much determined by convenience and custom as by logic. If some crops are spaced wider than they normally demand this can be made up by planting closer in the rows, and also of course by a greater use of the space between the rows for interplanting. Like many gardeners, I have now gone metric and have rows 28cm (11in) wide with 52cm (20½in) between them, making a total of 80cm (31½in)

between each row. I find the small amount of extra width a definite advantage.

3. The space between the rows remains barren and of poor quality. This need not be quite true, as will be shown later in the chapter on green manure. My own feeling is that generally speaking the great advantages of building up this concentrated channel of rich composted growing medium for your principle crops far outweighs the minor disadvantages.

A great many variations on this rotation are possible, and a few are shown below.

This is shown more clearly in the diagram opposite from which it can be seen that the *sine qua non* of this rotation is the broad bean, for it is the only seed that can be sown late enough in the autumn to follow late summer

Crop	Sow/Plant	Harvest
Potato Runner bean Maincrop peas Cauliflower Tomato Onions	Spring/early summer	Autumn
Sprouts Broccoli Sprouting broccoli Kale Swede Celery Celeriac Leek Beet	Summer	Up to following spring
Broad beans Hardy peas Spring cabbage Spring lettuce	Autumn	Early the following summer

crops, germinate, grow through the winter, and produce a crop by the end of it. It is a legume, and so it fixes nitrogen, is virtually disease free, and is exceptionally easy to grow. It is true that the hardy pea has similar advantages but it cannot compare with the bean for reliability and usefulness, either as an edible crop or as a producer of green manure. Also, of course, the field, or tic, bean has many similarities to the broad bean, and many similar advantages; its disadvantage is that to produce a crop it has to stay in the ground until very late in the summer

and this limits the choice of crops that can follow it.

The above description may give the impression that we are leaving a fair proportion of the garden infertile, but this is not exactly the case. Our aim is eventually to get the whole of it into a highly fertile condition. What we are doing is to ensure that when there is a limited amount of compost available, as tends to be the case, especially in the early stages, then the heavy feeders get priority.

Notice, too, that this rotation is far

Crop	January	February	March	April	May	June	July	August	September	October	November	December	January	February	March	April	May	June	July	August
New Potato																				
Maincrop Potato																				
Runner Bean																				
Maincrop Pea																				
Summer Cauliflower																				
Tomato																				
Onion																				
Broad Bean																				
Celery																				
Celeriac																				
Sprouts																				
Winter Cauliflower																				
Sprouting Broccoli																				
Kale																				
Cabbages																				
Leek																				
Parsnip																				
Salsify																				
Scorzonera																				
Salsify for Greens																				
Spinach Beet																				
Seakale Beet																				
Spring Cabbage																				
Hardy Peas																				
Tic or Field Beans																				

easier to operate under a no-digging system. Digging is not excluded but care must be taken to maintain the line of the compost rows and retain the compost in them, which is not easy if you dig to any depth. This question of no-digging is examined briefly in Chapter 5.

You will realize by now that just as the broad bean occupies a dominant position in your crop rotation, so it will tend under this system to occupy a correspondingly dominant position in your diet. This is accentuated by the fact that it gives not one crop but three. First the tops should be picked off in

April or May as soon as three or four trusses of flowers have blossomed; this produces a useful, though unexciting, variation in the diet of greens that are dominant at this season. A few weeks later immature bean pods may be picked off when they are two or three inches long and cooked whole, or chopped up and eaten raw in salad; and lastly the familiar podded bean in June and July.

The system of having a fixed fertile strip and the whole question of crop rotation are discussed in full detail in my book *Planning the Organic Vegetable Garden* (Thorsons 1986).

CHAPTER 4
GREEN MANURE

As has been said already, all life on this planet derives ultimately from the ability of plants to use the energy of the sun to enable them to build up complex organic compounds which then either feed higher organisms or else decompose to create fertile soil. There is a third way in which plants benefit us: by storing the energy of the sun which would otherwise be radiated out into space and wasted. The importance of these three functions calls into question the time-honoured practice of aiming at a weed-free garden, an artificially maintained expanse of bare soil in which rows of selected plants are permitted to grow in isolation, living like monks or kings uncontaminated by the proximity of lesser mortals.

In addition, during the winter, when it is difficult to think of useful crops to grow, the ground is left bare so that frost can act upon it. Both these practices are in opposition to the need to maximize the use of the sun's energy, but this is a question that is very seldom given sufficient or even any consideration in organizing the garden or planning rotations. On a practical level it is an important factor in maintaining the fertility of the small garden, especially when organic material is hard to come by. So long as the soil is left bare its potential value as a converter or storer of the sun's energy is being wasted. As a general rule, therefore, all ground should be fully covered with growth for as much of the time as it practicable in order that the maximum amount of plant growth is achieved and the maximum amount of the sun's energy is used. What is not consumed by animals or humans is then returned to the soil to build up its fertility.

Leaving Fallow
Not many gardeners nowadays would be happy with the 'fallow year' technique where land is deliberately left uncropped to enable it to grow a mixed crop of weeds which are then turned back into the soil. If green manuring is going to be practised some method of integrating it into the general garden routine without sacrificing edible crops must be found. It is comparatively simple to grow a crop of some sort through the winter and this is far better than leaving the ground bare. Exposing the soil to frost, which is the main reason for leaving the soil bare, is effective in increasing its friability, particularly in the case of clay or silts, but this is only a physical rearrangement of what is already there, which is confined to the top few inches of soil and which effects no lasting improvement to the soil. Incorporating organic matter, however, actually changes the soil by altering its components and structure, and so helps to build up its long-term fertility.

The question of growing green manure crops between edible crops is more controversial because it may in some cases be detrimental to the growth of the edible crop. However, as with the fallow year, there is a time-honoured precedent in the undersowing of grain crops with clover and similar practices.

There are four main opportunities for growing green manure crops: the first is to sow catch crops where the land is temporarily vacant between lifting one crop and planting the next. The second is to undersow crops that will be removed and which will then be replaced by the already established green manure. The third is to sow it between summer crops where there is not enough space to intersow an edible crop. The fourth is to sow it on vacant ground over the winter.

Fenugreek
For the first, the traditional crop is mustard. This has a disadvantage that it is a brassica and could increase the vulnerability to club root. A better choice is fenugreek, which is not so prolific of green growth but which is a legume and thus fixes nitrogen, and which is also edible (at least the Indians think so!) It only has one problem which may affect some gardens. Its ability to fix nitrogen depends upon the presence in the soil of a nitrogen-fixing bacteria which attaches itself and breeds on its roots. If this bacteria is absent the nitrogen fixing operation will not take place and the plant's value as a green manure crop is much less. It is easy to check because the bacteria breeds in small pale nodules on the roots. If the nodules are absent your soil is almost certainly deficient in the bacteria and the usual procedure is to procure an inocula. Unfortunately it is expensive and at present is not available on less than a farm scale (£6-8 per 25 kilograms of seed). For the small gardener the best thing is to beg, borrow or steal

a few plants of lucerne from a farmer and transplant them in your garden, checking as you do so that the lucerne plants have the tell-tale nodules on their roots. Lucerne (known outside farming circles as alfalfa) is also a legume and shares the same nitrogen-fixing bacteria as fenugreek.

Fenugreek seed is occasionally obtainable from seed merchants for sprouting, but is much more cheaply bought from Indian shops (sometimes under its Indian name of *mehte*) where it is sold as a flavouring for cooking. If used for green manuring it should be cropped as soon as it begins to flower. It will produce a crop within eight weeks and so it may be used to fill in a gap where there is not sufficient time to grow an edible crop. As well as being sown when land is vacant it can be sown between crops in their early stages because normally the distance between rows is determined by their eventual size or by the needs of access. There is no reason at all, for instance, why the space between peas or beans whose purpose is mainly to allow you to pick them, should not be carpeted with a green manure crop rather than left bare.

There are occasions when a catch crop of this sort should not be sown: for instance, where it will compete for food or moisture with edible crops; where an edible catch crop might be sown instead, or where a more valuable long-term green manure ought to be sown.

Anyone who is capable of forward planning, and who bears in mind that bare earth, or ground covered with unproductive weeds, is land that is not being used to its full potential, will be continually finding places that can safely and profitably be sown in this way.

Undersowing or Intersowing
The main use for this is with crops that

will be lifted during the winter when it is too late to resow the ground, a technique that is particularly applicable to brassicas (sprouts, broccoli, cauliflowers, cabbages etc). Some time after planting should elapse to allow the brassicas to establish themselves and put out a root system: in reasonable weather (not too hot and dry) a period of about three weeks should be enough. Here is a list of green manure crops that can be used and their sowing times. There are several other green manure crops that could be sown to give variety, but it seems better to not overload people with complicated choices.

If you are using the fixed-row system

Plant main crop	Sow green manure	Green manure crop
Late June to July	Mid-July to early August	Clover (preferably Crimson clover, *trifolium incarnatum*) Melilot (sometimes known as Sweet clover) Lucerne (known as Alfalfa)
August	Late August to September	Winter tares Hungarian Rye

described in the last chapter, then it will normally be necessary to wait until the intermediate (summer) crop is lifted before sowing the green manure crop, and to try and make these coincide.

For sowing after September you will have to fall back on the good old broad bean, which quite apart from its edible crop is a serious contender for the green manure championship title. A word of warning is needed here though: it is important to understand that beans sown as green manure are treated as green manure and not clung on to in order to get a crop of beans in July, or the whole cropping routine of your garden will go to ruin. It takes quite a lot of character to ruthlessly lift row upon row of broad bean plants in May knowing that in only a month or two they will be producing a handsome crop; but it must be done.

We are now in a position to reconstruct the rotation shown in the last chapter, filling in the contribution that green manuring can make without interfering with the cropping. I should like to emphasize again that this is not a gardening book, and this does not represent a full rotation or even necessarily an ideal one: it merely illustrates the sort of rotation that can be worked out (see overleaf).

How to Use the Crop

We now need to consider what we do with our green manure crop when we have grown it. There are two main choices: either we remove it and use it on the compost heap, or we turn it into the ground where it is. There are two dangers with the latter: one has already been mentioned, that, if the proportion of carbon is too high, there will be a danger of nitrogen starvation. This can be guarded against by using green manure crops with a high nitrogen content, such as legumes, and also by

9in (23cm) Principal Crop	21in (55cm) Intersown Crop	
	Edible Crop	**Green Manure Crop**
YEAR 1 Spring Plant maincrop potatoes	Spring cabbage (planted last autumn)	May be possible to intersow with fenugreek as cabbages are lifted
May		
June	Finish lifting spring cabbage	
July	Transplant 2 rows lettuce, etc.	
August		
Autumn Lift potatoes, sow triple rows broad beans		Sow 4 rows broad beans for green manuring
Winter		
YEAR 2 Spring	Sow turnips, summer cabbage, kohl rabi, radish (brassicas)	Hoe off broad beans
June Hoe off broad beans		
July Plant sprouts or other brassicas		
Autumn		Sow winter tares
Winter		
YEAR 3 Spring Lift sprouts. Sow parsnips, salsify	Sow summer vegetables (not brassicas)	Hoe off winter tares as ground is needed
May		
June		
July		
August		
Autumn		
Winter	Transplant winter lettuces, spring cabbage	
Year 4 Spring Lift parsnips. Plant maincrop potatoes		

For future years either repeat the above or use a similar rotation.

never allowing them to grow to a point where they become woody or seedy. The second danger has yet to be mentioned since it never occurs when applying compost to the garden, but it can do so with green manure, and that is an excess of nitrogen. The effect of this will be again to stimulate very energetic bacterial activity which will use up the carbon in the soil. A proportion of the carbon will be converted to carbon dioxide and taken up into the atmosphere, and this will deplete the organic content and fertility of the soil. This will not immediately affect plant growth but will affect the long-term maintenance of the soil structure.

The fact is that in nature there is a process of growth and decay which is never static but which maintains a reasonably balanced and stable continuity. You are engaged in increasing its efficiency of action, but if you do this abruptly you are bound to upset the dynamic balance of the soil and this has the danger of disrupting the whole process.

On these grounds I think that generally it is better to decompose green manure crops in the compost heap rather than turn them into the top soil. There are exceptions, though. For instance if you are trying to improve a very heavy soil, one technique is to grow legumes with a considerable root system (clover, lucerne). Hoe them off at ground level and leave the roots to rot in the ground. Legumes have a reasonable balance between nitrogen and carbon, and the roots will rot down *in situ* leaving an intricate network of little channels which will help aeration and drainage and improve the physical condition of the soil.

There is an important distinction between the two methods of using green manure explained above. If you turn green manure into the soil where it was grown you are increasing the fertility of the soil. If you take the crop off to the compost heap you are temporarily reducing the fertility of the soil where you grew it, and if you then use the compost elsewhere you are permanently doing so. In this case you must be careful to make up for that loss when you are next sowing or planting.

Whilst on the subject of green manure it is worth mentioning a few plants which it is worth growing for their contribution to the compost heap, quite apart from any other value they may have:

Jerusalem artichokes. The tops can be cut off in July at about four to five feet to stop them blowing over. The remainder of the stem should be cut in the autumn after it has gone brown and is rather less useful.

Sunflower. The whole plant is very good food for compost; it is better cut when green. They may be grown very close together in some out-of-the-way patch and will still produce sizeable flowers.

Sweetcorn. As grown on the farm for silage sweet corn produces up to forty tons per acre between May and August, but this of course depends upon growing plants very close together, though even so they will still produce eatable cobs.

Comfrey. Comfrey is probably the most valuable producer of compost material there is, but it does have some disadvantages. It occupies a site permanently; it is very difficult to get rid of; and although it can be eaten in various ways, it is not an edible crop that finds favour with many. It has a carbon/nitrogen ratio as low as 10:1 which means that it can be used as an activator for the compost heap. It also means it can be crushed and laid direct in trenches in place of compost. As it also has a high potash content it is valuable used in this way for crops that need potash such as potatoes, beans, etc. Comfrey should be planted in any damp out-of-the-way part of the garden, but it needs looking after. Nettles or couch grass will smother it, so it must be kept weeded as far as perennials are concerned. It will smother most summer annuals and to aid this it should be planted closer together than is usually advocated – 15in (40cm) is a good distance. Plants or root cuttings should be planted at any time of the year except in mid-winter, but preferably in the spring.

Comfrey likes a deep rich soil and will repay dressings of manure or fertilizer. It is quite a good way of converting raw or even chemical fertilizer into an organic compost.

Nettles make excellent compost. If you wish to get rid of them you cut them three or four times a year and in two years they should die out. If you wish to keep them as a provider of compost material (some people think they are good to eat too) cut them only twice a year.

Bracken can be eliminated in the same way and, as it is spreading rapidly and all set to become a major weed pest, you are doing the environment a favour by cutting it down. It is valuable compost material as it has a very high potash content, especially if it is cut young, but it is rather difficult to handle in the heap, for four reasons.

Firstly, the amount of stalk in comparison to green leaf is much higher than in most other plants. Secondly, the stalk is quite hard and does not compost down easily unless it is chopped into small pieces. Thirdly, the stalk is very dry and is reluctant to absorb moisture so that if you try to water it the water tends to run off and drain through towards the bottom of the heap, which then becomes waterlogged. And lastly it

is very springy and too much of it may make your heap so open that it won't heat up. However much you bang it down or jump on it it springs up again like a trampoline, apparently unaffected.

As most heaps cannot maintain their heat because they rapidly compact down, it is theoretically possible to achieve a balance whereby there is enough bracken in the heap to delay its compacting, but not so much that it is too open to heat up. In practice it isn't too easy to achieve this, but it is worth experimenting by alternating narrow layers of bracken between thicker ones of garden rubbish to weigh it down.

I have just learned that bracken spores, active from mid-July to mid-September, are carcinogenic and that throughout the growing season – from May to October – the whole plant may be very toxic. If you think of composting bracken on any scale it would be wise to check with the leading authority in this country, Professor Jim Taylor at Aberystwyth University.

Rough Grass is not a very good material to use in quantity in the compost heap; it is very slow to break down and the guillotine process when you are turning is made very difficult. It is best stacked in some out of the way corner on its own and left to rot down anaerobically over a long period.

Weeds

Weeds themselves are of course a green manure and can be used as such. Under natural conditions the mixture of crops will adjust itself to the soil and in some cases will act to rectify the soil's deficiencies: for example, daisies flourish in acid soil and are rich in calcium which, if the plants are allowed to rot down *in situ*, will counteract the acidity. For this reason many people advocate encouraging weeds in certain circumstances, but there are two objections to this; the first is that nature is in no hurry; her time scale is measured in millions of years whereas we think in terms of decades, years, or seasons. The effect of a natural weedcrop in one season could be very small, and which of us is prepared to wait longer?

The second objection is that there is no reason to believe that any habitat under natural conditions will revert to a state that is specially beneficial to the human race or to the crops that we wish to grow or to the methods that we wish to use. Generally speaking, therefore, it is better to aim for a green manure crop that we believe has specially beneficial

qualities. There is only one reservation here, and that is that very little study has been made of green manures, and beyond a small amount of rule-of-thumb knowledge, such as the advantages of using legumes, we do not really know what are the best methods. If this country is to become more vegetarian in its diet and in the uses it makes of the land, and if at the same time it is to avoid the increasing use of chemical fertilizers, it is a matter of some urgency to carry out research and experiment in this direction.

Poor Soil
Sometimes when a patch of soil is particularly poor it is decided not to

Here is a list of suitable crops for different needs:

Plant	Sow	In ground	Benefits
Lupin	Spring	2 months or longer	Bulky material, excellent for light acid soils Nitrogen fixers
Melilot or Lucerne	Spring or early Autumn	18 months	Deep rooting system for clay soils Nitrogen fixers
Rye	Up to end of September	Until following spring	Fastest growing winter hardy crop
Tares	Up to end of September	Until following spring	Nitrogen fixer
Fenugreek	Any time, but not hardy	8-10 weeks	Nitrogen fixer
Mustard	Any time, but not hardy	6-8 weeks	Good for potatoes because it suppresses potato eelworm

crop it for a time, but to concentrate entirely on green manures in order to improve its fertility.

Several different schemes for this are recommended in different books. Which one you practice depends very much on circumstances. It is no good trying to grow a crop like sweetcorn, which is a fairly heavy feeder; so the best thing is to grow a catch crop of mustard or fenugreek and turn it into the soil after six or eight weeks to produce a base for some further crop. If you start late in the season your choice is limited to rye or winter tares but at other times you can choose between lupins for rapid production of bulk, deep-rooted melilot for clay soils, and crimson clover which will produce a huge amount of greenery and a very attractive crop of flowers after fifteen months.

CHAPTER 5
ORGANIC FERTILIZERS

This chapter is concerned with organic fertilizers that, strictly speaking, are rather outside the subject of composting. A garden that has been well supplied with compost over a period will rarely require additional fertilizers, so compost gardeners should normally have little need for them. That said, it takes some time to build up the fertility of a run-down soil and during this period there will certainly be occasions when an addition of concentrated nutrient is needed. Even when your soil has reached a very fertile level there may well be times when a boost is beneficial – for example, a harsh spring may call for nitrogen for spring vegetables; peas, beans, potatoes, onions may suffer from a shortage of potash after continuous heavy rain. So it seems appropriate to give a brief resumé of the various organic fertilizers that are available.

It is not easy to distinguish fertilizers from composts, manures and so on as there is no clear-cut demarcation between them. A rule-of-thumb distinction is that fertilizers are used primarily for their nutrient content and do not directly benefit the soil structure, whereas manures and compost have a much smaller nutrient content than fertilizers and are the principal means by which we are able to maintain (and improve) the soil structure. However, if compost is applied regularly in sufficient quantity it is normally sufficient to maintain the soil in a fertile state both as regards nutrients and soil structure.

First, a word about organic fertilizers in general. Most nutrients are assimilated by plants with the take-up of water from the soil and for this to happen the nutrients themselves must be water-soluble. Most organic fertilizers, however, as opposed to inorganic ones, hold their nutrients in complex molecules that are not water-soluble and are therefore not immediately available to plants. It is the action of micro-organisms in the soil that makes them become water-soluble. This conversion of insoluble nutrients to soluble ones can continue to operate over a considerable period (in the case of bristles or horse-hair, for example, the release of soluble nitrogen may last for five years or longer). Inorganic fertilizers being, generally speaking, more water-soluble, will have a much more immediate effect but will also be quicker to leach out of the soil. As compared with organic fertilizers they tend to be quick-acting but short-lived.

If you want quick results from organic fertilizers they must be applied in a situation that is favourable to the micro-organisms that are going to convert them to a soluble form. It is no good, therefore, merely scattering them on the dry surface of the soil. And, as they are insoluble in water, it isn't much good scattering them on the surface and then attempting to water them in either. They need to be worked into the top few inches of the soil where micro-organisms flourish. Bacteria work best in a soil that is damp, warm, well-aerated and which contains a sufficient quantity of lime. Applications of fertilizer in cold weather or to a very dry or very compacted soil will produce very little immediate benefit.

Another factor affecting the speed of action of organic fertilizers is the fineness of the particles. A coarse-grained texture will act more slowly and, correspondingly, will last longer.

Fertilizers, being concentrated, are used in very much smaller quantities than compost and one problem is the difficulty of judging the amount required and spreading it evenly. A handful of fertilizer may weigh anything between 1½ to 3oz (42-85g) according to the size of your hand and how you fill it. Spreading this evenly over say, a square yard is far from easy. If you are not accustomed to using fertilizers it is probably a good idea to take four average handfuls, weigh them and divide by four to get an idea how much each one of your handfuls weighs. Then, to simplify the spreading, mix one handful of fertilizer with three of sand or sandy soil of roughly the same particle size and then spread four times as much of the mixture. For example, if your hand holds 2oz (55g) of the fertilizer and you need to apply it at a rate of 4oz per square yard (115g per 0.83m²), then for every square yard you take two handfuls of fertilizer and six of sand, mix them thoroughly, and then spread this a handful at a time (eight handfuls) over the area.

Fertilizer is very often dribbled in a band 2 to 4in (5-10cm) wide alongside the row and about 2in (5cm) from the stem of the plants, rather than being spread evenly over a whole area. Do this on a calm day and work it into the topsoil as you go. If the topsoil is at all dry it should be watered so as to encourage the growth of the bacteria that are to perform the service of converting it to soluble forms. If fertilizer accidentally spills onto the leaves of plants, water the plant as soon as possible to wash it off and normally no harm will result. In such cases organic fertilizers are not nearly so likely to scorch young plants as inorganic ones.

Use of Fertilizers

Speaking generally, leaf-producing plants benefit from a high level of nitrogen in the soil. In the case of slow-growing plants such as Brussels sprouts and winter cabbage this should be in a slow-release form. For summer vegetables it should be in a relatively quick-release form. It is a good practice to give spring crops (for example, spring cabbage, over-wintered spinach beet, and so on) a boost of quick-acting nitrogen as soon as they begin to show spring growth. Root crops require a good supply of phosphates, especially in the seedling stage. Too much nitrogen will lead to an excess of leaf growth. Some of them, especially potatoes, also need a supply of potash. All plants that produce a seed or fruit crop benefit mostly from a potash fertilizer and to a lesser extent from phosphates. A soil heavily manured with nitrogen may actually depress yields. It may also inhibit the valuable nitrogen fixation of peas and beans. Potash applied in the autumn has the effect of ripening the new season's growth on fruit trees, roses, etc, and is therefore especially valuable for those that fruit or flower on the previous season's growth.

Dried blood contains 7 to 14 per cent nitrogen and can be applied at a rate of 2 to 4oz per square yard (65-135g per square metre) to leaf-producing plants that need a fairly rapid supply of nitrogen. It is the most water-soluble and therefore readily available of all organic fertilizers.

Hoof and horn meal contains about 10 to 14 per cent nitrogen. It is slow-acting so it is useful for plantings that require steady feeding over a long period (winter brassicas, for example). The speed at which it becomes available depends on the fineness of the grist. It also contains some phosphate, the amount of which varies up to 10 per cent according to the formulation.

Bone meal contains about 20 per cent phosphorus and a small amount of nitrogen (up to 5 per cent). It is slow-acting and a coarse grade will continue to act over a period of two to three years.

Bone flour, which is a by-product of glue manufacture, is much less available now that most glues are produced synthetically. It contains about 25 per cent phosphates that are in a much more rapidly available form than bone meal.

Fish meal is manufactured from fish waste and its nutrient composition varies. It can be up to 10 per cent nitrogen and 14 per cent phosphate. It also contains a large variety of trace elements and more humus than most fertilizers. It is therefore half-way between a fertilizer and a manure. It is often fortified with inorganic potash so that it can be used as a balanced fertilizer.

Seaweed meal is made from dried seaweed pulverized to a fine grist. It contains up to 2 per cent potash and 2 per cent nitrogen and is about the best source of organic potash. It also contains a wide variety of trace elements. In its liquid form it can be sprayed directly onto plants, which is sometimes more effective than applying fertilizers to the ground. So long as you avoid doing it in full sunshine it will not do any harm and can sometimes be a spectacular life-saver to plants that look sickly (see also seaweed, pages 106-107).

Wood ash is organic in the sense that it is derived from living matter, but burning has replaced the complex organic molecules by simple minerals. The potash is in a highly soluble form and in sandy soils will leach out very quickly. The potash content is very variable, depending on the plant material that was burned. The younger the plant material burned the higher the potash content. The average is about 10 per cent, though ash from young bracken can contain up to 50 per cent, but then bracken is such a valuable compost material it seems wasteful to just burn it. Wood ash also contains a high proportion of lime, which can be harmful to some soils and should not be used on soil that is already well-limed. It also contains a small quantity of sulphur, which can be poisonous to plants. Coal or coke ash are both much higher in sulphur and it is safer not to use these in the garden. It is really much better to add wood ash to your compost heap where it enables the potash to be converted to an organic form.

Soot, like wood ash, claims to be organic and, for the same reason, this claim is a little dubious. Household soot contains 4 to 6 per cent nitrogen, which is quickly released into the soil. Fresh soot contains sulphur and other poisons so it is best weathered by being exposed to the air under cover for two to three months before use. I don't know anyone who uses soot these days, so a friendly arrangement with your local chimney-sweep might produce as much nitrogen fertilizer as you're ever likely to need for free. It should also make a useful compost-heap activator, though I have never tried it. It is a deterrent to slugs, snails and other pests, who are said to dislike its smell. Soot should never be applied to freshly limed soil (nor, of course, lime to freshly sooted soil) as this leads to a chemical reaction and the nitrogen will be lost.

Epsom salts aren't organic either, but they are widely used by organic growers. They are the best cure for magnesium shortage. Magnesium deficiency retards growth and usually shows as a discolouring (yellow or broken) of the leaves between the veins, although it is not always easy to identify for certain. It occurs mostly in sandy soils, especially if they are allowed to become acid.

Epsom salts are best used as a foliar spray, mixed at a rate of 2oz to 2 gallons (6g per litre) of water. A horticultural grade of Epsom salts is available at most garden centres.

Dolomite is ground limestone rock composed of calcium carbonate and magnesium carbonate and is a more permanent cure for magnesium deficiency. However, it cannot be used for a magnesium deficiency on an alkaline soil which, though rare, is not unknown. It is a natural produce – that is, a natural rock. It is accepted as 'organic' because it is not water-soluble and only becomes available to plants as a result of the action of micro-organisms in the soil.

Calcified seaweed is not, strictly speaking, a sea weed: it is an animal growth, similar to coral, that multiplies itself on the seabed. It is dredged and ground to a fine whiteish powder. It contains slow-release magnesium in addition to calcium and a variety of trace elements.

As a substitute for lime it is rather expensive but, as well as its ability to maintain the correct degree of acidity in the soil, it has valuable properties as a fertilizer. However, like peat, it is a dwindling resource that is being exploited regardless of the future and this poses a problem for all of us who are concerned that our methods should stand the test of time.

Lime is, of course, not an organic fertilizer either, it is a chemical that, like dolomite, occurs naturally in rock. It contains a high proportion of calcium and its main function is not as a fertilizer but as a soil conditioner to correct the acidity of the soil. Most plants grow best in a soil that is slightly acid, but most soils tend to become too acid as calcium leaches out of the soil, and this has to be corrected. The soluble form of lime, available in garden shops as hydrated lime, is very quick acting and short-lived and so organic growers prefer ground limestone which breaks down gradually and, consequently, is much longer-lasting. Calcified seaweed is even better for this purpose, but it is considerably more expensive. The acidity of the soil is important not only to plants but also to the organic gardener's unpaid labour force, the earthworms, who cannot live in an acid soil, so it is important to purchase a testing kit and to check the soil regularly. The degree of acidity of the soil is expressed as the pH value, and the kit is sometimes known as a pH tester (see page 55.)

CHAPTER 6
ODDS AND ENDS

New Soil

I am always sorry for people inheriting new land or a building plot to whom the following advice is given: 'double dig the plot from end to end. Remove all perennial weeds and every scrap of root; remove all stones, bits of metal, plastic, old bricks, broken glass, broken-down concrete mixers; incorporate a barrowload of manure every four yards, etc., etc.' They must feel as daunted as Hercules did when he first heard about the twelve labours.

I think most gardening writers make very heavy weather of this situation, just as they make heavy weather of the problem of weeds. Of course if your garden really is situated on top of builders' rubble or an old rubbish dump you will have a few problems. However, as this is not strictly speaking a compost problem, and as I have never had personal experience of it, I am going to pass that one by and assume that you have soil of some sort that is capable of being worked and of growing plants. Here is a method that will enable you to grow crops quickly, and should considerably cut down the amount of slog involved.

First of all scythe or cut down the grass and weeds to soil level. Then mark out your row and slice off the turf in neat blocks a spade's width right the way down it. You now have a band of bare top soil, very matted and perhaps quite hard and possibly also full of perennial roots. What you do next depends upon the nature of the soil, the nature of the topgrowth and what you are going to grow. If the soil is completely full of perennial roots (couch grass, thistle, ground elder, etc) then you will have to dig a trench about six inches deep, take the soil away and burn it. Once burnt, the soil can be brought back, mixed with compost and replaced, or clean soil with or without compost can be brought in from elsewhere. If you have only just moved in and have no compost, you will have to go out and buy some on this one and (with luck) only occasion. If you have a clay soil you can grow crops which require some feeding provided you can create a reasonable surface tilth to get them started. Runner beans would be a good crop, sown initially in a box or pots and transplanted individually with compost. Or, later in the season, brassicas transplanted similarly. Kale and savoys are two brassicas that are fairly undemanding as regards soil fertility. If the soil is light, or looks very poor, try to incorporate some organic matter and grow a crop which does not require very heavy feeding, for example spinach beet, beet, turnips or swedes. Do not grow potatoes by this method as you will have difficulty with earthing them up.

Making use of the turf

The turf you have removed can either

Note for Plates 6, 7 and 8

These plates show how to use an opaque mulch (plastic, newspaper or carpet), together with limited amounts of compost, to get an immediate crop from rough, unbroken land, and at the same time suppress all weeds so that, by the following season, the soil is comparatively easy to clean. I do not claim that this is necessarily better than normal procedures for breaking in new ground, but it does save labour and enables you to grow crops in new ground with the least possible delay.

I used this method on my allotment, shown in Plate 5. Half the allotment I cultivated in the normal way to grow summer crops, winter root crops, and so on, the other half I left for brassicas to be planted out in July. I decided to use a carpet mulch because I had some old stair carpet 80 cm (31½ inches) wide, which is just the distance between rows that I prefer.

Plate 7

The carpet is now turned back, a trowel hole is made in the centre of the composted plant position, the hole is filled with water and left to drain (*top left*). The transplant with its ball of soil is put loosely into the hole and the carpet laid flat again so that the plant can be positioned with its stem aligned exactly against the carpet (*below*). The plant is then firmed in so that the soil comes up to the transplant's first true leaves (*top right*) and the carpet is put back into position.

Plate 7

Plate 8

Plate 8

The photograph, *top,* shows how the plants shown in Plate 7 are doing a month later. They are growing well now but there are signs of trouble ahead, indicated by the reddish tinge on some of the older leaves. Later they did show symptoms of nitrogen deficiency. This is because the roots outgrew the composted area and were searching in the arid soil outside it for sustenance. However, we are getting a sufficient crop from the area to have made it worthwhile growing the crops and, as can be seen from the picture, there are no weeds. Next spring the ground should be fairly clean, though the mulch will not have smothered some of the perennials like, in this instance, the bracken. These will have to be continually broken or hoed off until the roots are exhausted, which may take three or four years.

The picture *below* shows rows of cauliflowers and celery, similarly mulched, but this time the mulch is newspaper held down by an inch or so of soil. I have left the area between the rows for weeds to grow and, every now and again I cut them down to provide compost material.

be stacked in a turf pile and allowed to rot down anaerobically for at least a year (this is in fact one of the occasions when an anaerobic heap is a better alternative to an aerobic one). It is a variation of the Chinese 'earth compost heap' described on page 22. Stack the turves neatly like courses of bricks, turf side downwards. Leave the top flat and finish it off with a layer of soil in which is sown a green manure crop such as clover.

One problem with turf heaps is wireworms. Wireworms are the larvae of the click beetle and are up to ¾in (2cm) long with shiny bodies, pale brown to yellow in colour. There are a great many of them in turf and grassland, up to 3,000,000 per acre (0.4 ha), which works out at about 600 per square yard (0.8m) of topsoil. This seems an awful lot and it does seem rather hard to believe, but then my mind also boggles at the fact (quoted by Sir John Russell in his *Soil Conditions and Plant Growth*) that 'a saltspoonful of dried soil contains up to 6,000 million organisms.'

As these little creatures have a very bad press in gardening circles, I feel I must say a word on their behalf, for left alone they are great benefactors of mankind. In a natural state they are major contributors to the process by which the fertility of undisturbed grassland increases year by year. Their preferred diet is the dead roots of grass, which they convert into humus, at the same time creating both space and a receptive soil for new roots to grow. It is only when mankind comes along and ploughs up the grassland that they are forced to change their diet to potatoes and the roots of whatever crops they can find. They have no other option except to starve. They have voracious appetites and do nothing except eat. They cannot even breed as at the end of

four years they pupate and turn into click beetles and the pleasures and responsibilities of propagating the species rest with them.

When you make a turf heap this seething population becomes concentrated into a limited area with a diminishing food supply. Many die – probably the great majority – but those that can emigrate will choose fruitful soil where potatoes and the roots of lettuces, tomatoes and most other vegetables abound. One way of dealing with this, I have heard, is to make your turf heap on a sheet of plastic, which effectively blocks their escape route and so they starve. Another method is to sow green manure crops of mustard, although opinions seem to differ about the effect of mustard on wireworms. Lawrence Hills in *Grow Your Own Fruit and Vegetables* says that wireworms eat mustard so avidly that they complete their four-year cycle in a month or so, pupate, turn into click beetles and fly away to lay their eggs on someone else's land where, with any luck, the farmer, not being an organic grower, will slaughter them with pesticides. I must admit I have doubts about the ethics of this, and anyway an old Ministry of Agriculture advisory leaflet seems to contradict it all with the somewhat cryptic statement, 'It is sometimes supposed that mustard has some effect on wireworms, apart from causing starvation, and . . . this possibility cannot be neglected for wireworms are most difficult to starve . . .'. To confuse us further an updated leaflet does not mention mustard at all but confines itself to a list of pesticides! However, as the subject of this book is compost and not pest control I refer you to the many books that have sections on pest control and give advice on how to trap wireworms and other methods of control.

If the turves are full of perennial weeds you have another problem. If they are not too pernicious and too numerous you may decide to go ahead with the turf heap. In that case, rather than sowing a green manure crop, it may be better to wrap the heap in plastic held down by bricks. If they are pernicious perennials such as ground elder you would do better to put them in your aerobic heap so long as you are confident that it will heat up sufficiently. If not, it would be safer to burn them and put the ash on the heap.

Alternatively the turves can be laid upside down alongside the original cut so that they cover over the turf between the cut rows. At this point there are several courses open to you, depending on the condition of the turves:

• if the turves are quite fertile and reasonably free of perennial roots you may wish to try intercropping an edible crop. Make a fairly large hole with a trowel and fill it with compost and sow or plant the crop in that.

• if the turves are too full of weeds for this, then you can sprinkle a layer of soil on top and sow a green manure crop. A possible programme would be to sow fenugreek, after about two months hoe it off, cover it with another shallow layer of soil and sow mustard. By this process the soil and double layer of turf will have gone a long way towards decomposition over the summer months.

• on the other hand, the turves may be so full of weeds that it is hardly practicable to grow a green manure crop in them. In this case the best plan is to cover them with a mulch of newspaper, black plastic or old stair carpet, or any other opaque material that can be laid flat to cover over the weeds. A newspaper mulch is in many ways the best as it does not attract slugs (black plastic is particularly bad in this

respect) but it is more trouble, and in the end not very attractive to look at. It should be laid thickly: a complete newspaper should be folded to the right width and laid with each paper overlapping the next by a fair margin. Papers without much bulk may have to be doubled. The paper should then be held down by stones, although to begin with this will not look very elegant. In time, however, it loses its garishness and blends in. It takes an awful lot of stones and you must be generous or you will find your newspaper blowing about and tearing in the first strong wind. A better way of holding the papers down is to lay a strip of black plastic over them. Black plastic can now be bought rolled in long strips from garden centres. This requires much less weighting down, and if you sprinkle a dusting of lime between the paper and the plastic this will effectively deter the slugs. Perhaps the best cover of all is a 1in (2.5cm) layer of soil, and this is shown in the photograph on page 60.

Probably the best and simplest mulch is an old stair carpet 21in (53cm) wide, if you have or can get hold of it. Poor quality ones that have failed to sell at auction can sometimes be obtained free at the end of the auction. It does not have to be made from organic fibre as we are not expecting it to rot down and become part of the compost. In fact, a carpet of man-made fibres is probably an advantage because it won't rot down and therefore can be used again and again.

As I have said I don't much like using black plastic on its own. Apart from the slug problem it often tears and then weeds grow out of it. Its advantage is that it is fairly easy to tuck it in at the sides and hold it in place with soil.

If you are going to operate the 'fixed row' system, the cuts will be cleared of turf about 9in (23cm) wide with 21in

I ran out of carpet for my brassicas and finished the patch off with a newspaper mulch. In many ways newspapers are easier to lay than carpets – but you will need an awful lot of newspapers and quite a lot of soil (or an enormous number of stones) to hold them down satisfactorily. Note that I am using it at least six pages thick (three pages folded once). This paper probably will not rot down (or if it does it will take three or four years to do so) but the sheets will coagulate together to form a hard board, which you may have to remove and burn the following season, though if you are a fanatical recycler you could shred it to use as compost.

(53cm) between them, so there will not be enough turves to cover the whole space between the cuts. In fact, you will only be able to cover alternate spaces. What you will have is the following situation:

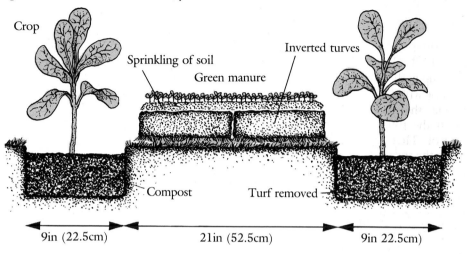

INTERPLANTING GREEN MANURE

So, what about the space which does not have inverted turves? One alternative of course is to slice the turves off here as well, invert them and treat them as the others with an intercrop or a green manure crop. But this means a lot more work and this is what we are trying to avoid. What we are trying to do is to get this plot into use with the least possible delay and the least amount

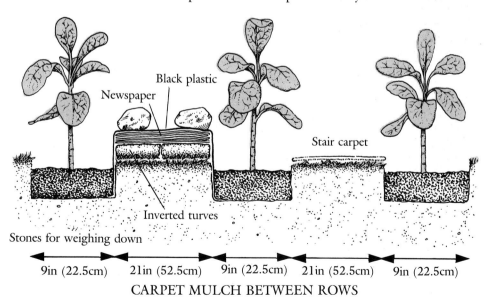

CARPET MULCH BETWEEN ROWS

of work. I think, therefore, it is better to mulch these alternate spaces as described above. Your situation is now like this:

Of course by this method you are not producing a perfect weed-free crop. Grass will sprout out from the edge of your turves. Docks will grow through the top. A whole variety of weeds will grow up in the trench beside your crop. Do not worry. About once a fortnight during the growing season just go down the rows keeping things under control. Hoe down the trench. Cut down the sprouting sides with shears or a very sharp spade. Pull off any dock leaves to stop them taking over. If you have some compost by now start to fill up the trenches. Half an hour spent once a fortnight will give you a good start on the long process of getting your garden so that it is not infested with really tiresome weeds. Meanwhile you are growing a crop, you are beginning to make compost, your green manure plants are working on the soil.

It may have occurred to you that the newspaper mulch technique is in total opposition to the idea put forward that the soil should always be growing something, that there should never be a bare patch. Nothing could be barer than several thicknesses of newspaper. Yes, that is true but the fact is there is no ideal way of gardening, no method that produces the best of all possible worlds in every respect. How you garden is a compromise, or a synthesis if you prefer, of a whole variety of different, and often opposing needs. You should indeed keep your ground growing and working for you as much as you can, but sometimes other needs prevail.

Liquid Manure

In days gone by it was recommended to hang a sack of cow manure in a 20 gallon (91 litre) barrel of water for a month; this produced a thick, scummy liquid which one then diluted down 1 pt (0.5 litre) in 3 pts (1.7 litres), and applied near to but not actually on the plants. It is hardly surprising one was advised to keep this dubious concoction away from plant stems and roots, for its strength and maturity were very haphazard and indeed hazardous. Nowadays a similar process is recommended using plants, notably comfrey or nettles or a mixture of the two. Nettles will give a more nitrogenous mixture, and comfrey one richer in potassium. The process is to get a twenty or forty gallon drum, and stuff it with plant material up to a foot from the top. Then fill it up with water (preferably rain water) so that the green material is just covered, and leave it for a month, stirring occasionally, when it can be used undiluted on any of the crops that require feeding.

This can be quite a valuable treatment for plants that require continuous feeding, for example outdoor tomatoes in July and August, celery, marrow, etc. If you are going to apply it in dry weather, it is important to water the plants very thoroughly first. And again, keep it away from actual contact with stems and foliage.

Sawdust Toilet

A major source of animal manure is human excreta, but in this country the great majority of this is wasted. One reason often given for this is that it can carry disease. Polio germs for instance will live for two weeks and jaundice can remain infective for considerably longer. But if proper composting methods are used there is no likelihood of any danger. In China human waste has been used to produce compost for over 4,000 years. (See Chinese 'earth compost', page 22.) Research into this has been carried out by Liverpool School of

Tropical Medicine in conjunction with the Centre for Alternative Technology, but it was inconclusive. To be on the safe side don't use it for salad crops or for any vegetables that are to be eaten fresh, but keep it for a year and use it for runner beans, leeks, potatoes and similar crops.

The following method is described by Hugh Flatt and is reproduced by permission of *Practical Self-Sufficiency* where it first appeared. It is perhaps not a very easy one to practise in an urban or suburban setting, but should present no great problems to the country dweller, except that of getting accustomed to the idea.

'Thirty years ago an elderly woman, who lived in one of our farm cottages, walked three miles every morning during the school term to empty the "earth closet" buckets at the Primary School. One time she was ill for a few days, and as she was a good friend of mine, I offered to do the job to keep it for her. The system, if such it could be called, was a disgrace. The buckets were tipped at random in a corner field bordering on the village, where a sloppy, unhygienic, bad-smelling mess resulted. This confirmed my feeling that we should demonstrate a proper, wholesome recycling of human waste.

'We have lived on a farm for more than thirty years, where we have had bucket lavatories. We have had a number of visitors during the year, and often two families in the farmhouse; but have not used chemicals. We have used sawdust, or sawdust mixed with soil, in our buckets, adding some each time after use: it is absorbent and sweet-smelling. While it is best to use deciduous sawdust to avoid the resins from the conifers which do not allow it to compost quite so well, I realize this is not always easy to obtain. No disinfectants are ever used.

'A daily routine of emptying the buckets is carried out. The base for the compost heap should be in an area of soil (from which worms, bacteria and other soil life can arrive) and it is started with a layer of cut weeds, grass or straw. The contents of the bucket, after tipping, are covered adequately each time with such materials as will reduce to a minimum any unpleasant smell, and prevent direct access of flies to the sewage: suitable kitchen waste can be incorporated and from time to time a thin layer of soil spread over (say once in three weeks). If available a layer of farmyard manure can also be incorporated with advantage, but it is by no means essential. The width of the heap should be limited to three or four feet to keep it aerobic, and the length is variable according to space available and the size of the heap required before closing; the height of the heap should not be over three to four feet. I have not normally covered these compost heaps, but this could be advisable temporarily during a spell of constant rain which is causing anaerobic conditions. In a prolonged dry spell it can also become necessary to water a heap.

'After three or four months I close the heap and start another: I top up the finished heap with a good layer of green material or straw, finishing with a layer of soil. It is then left for about four months, and turned once (with a dung fork, moving it all from one end, just shifting it along a couple of feet). This gives it a final aeration and in three weeks or so a fresh-smelling, friable, biologically active compost is ready to spread on the garden: if a heap is not "working" well a little limestone or chalk may help.

'A "Bush Brother" back from Australia told me how, in the British township where he lived, the buckets were emptied at night by the Chinese from a neighbouring township; they never enquired what was done with the material. The British used to purchase vegetables from the Chinese, which they admitted were much better and finer specimens than those they could grow!

'Finally, just because one uses a system regarded as archaic, that is no reason for the "loo" to be dingy, cobwebby and unaesthetic: on the contrary, it is important for it to be bright, regularly whitewashed or decorated. One of ours is out-of-doors and my wife has organized a pleasant approach between flowers and herbs.'

Mulching

Generally speaking mulching has one or more of four purposes: to hold moisture; to suppress weeds; to protect from frost; and to supply nutrients or organic matter to perennial or other permanent plantings.

Mulching can be either localized, where, say, the area in the immediate vicinity of a fruit tree is mulched, or it can be spread over a whole bed. Whatever its purpose it generally has the effect of suppressing weed and other

Purpose	Plants	When	Material
To conserve moisture and suppress annual weeds	Roses, shrubs, soft fruit, asparagus, globe artichokes	April/May before the ground dries out	Peat, leafmould, compost, lawn mowings
Suppression of perennial weeds	All types	Anytime	Newspaper, plastic, carpet
Frost protection	Asparagus, globe artichoke, many shrubs, some flowers (e.g. dahlias)	Autumn	Straw, rough leafmould, bracken, green manure crop
To encourage a thriving worm population (see page 108)		Anytime	Rough compost
Protecting Muddy paths, especially in raised bed growing			Straw, sawdust

growth as well, so that widespread mulching acts against the precept that as far as practicable the land should be growing a crop of some sort as much of the time as possible. Therefore, although it undoubtedly has its value, widespread mulching does have its dangers.

For example the system of sawdust mulching, proposed by F. L. King, which involves very large areas of the garden being covered by a thick annual mulch of sawdust seems to me to suffer from this disadvantage; this system derives from the example of the forest floor, but in the forest summer sunlight is used to maximum effect by the wide spread of leaves, whereas in a well-mulched garden as much as ninety per cent of the area may be bare soil, or in this case bare sawdust, for much of the summer. Think for example, of a bed of young sprout plants planted out in July, the regular 2-2½ ft (0.6-0.7m) apart.

However, if you can get it, sawdust is a very good mulch for crops like gooseberries and soft fruit generally where the suppression of perennial weeds is important. It will not of course get rid of perennials that are already established, but will act as a deterrent to the growth of new ones.

For mulches for breaking in new ground, see plates 6, 7 and 8.

On the left-hand page is a list of other occasions when the need for mulching is well established.

Potting Compost

When a commercial grower talks about compost he is referring to potting compost. Just as in this book we have been concerned with using garden compost to improve the soil in which plants grow to maturity, so potting compost is used to replace the soil in order to grow seeds and seedlings until they are ready for transplanting. Growing seedlings in frames or greenhouses is a more artificial activity than growing plants in the garden; in the garden compost is mixed with soil to produce something that approximates to the sort of natural conditions that plants are accustomed to. In the greenhouse a far more artificial situation exists, when the soil and environment are carefully contrived to ensure maximum germination and survival.

The best seed and potting compost for the organic gardener should be made from the following mixture:

	parts (by volume)
Sifted compost	2
Irish sphagnum peat	2
Horticultural grit	1
Sifted soil	2

This potting compost of course will not be fully sterilized, for quite apart from the sifted soil (which can be omitted) the compost itself is unlikely to be totally sterilized through and through. There is therefore *some* danger of disease, especially of 'damping off' which is a fungus disease transmitted through the soil and which results in small seedlings collapsing overnight. Most large growers sterilize their compost for safety, but small gardeners do not and they usually get away with it. If you do have trouble with this you may have to buy in sterilized potting compost, but I do not know of any such which is fully organic.

Worm Compost

Worm compost is made principally by the action of manure worms (brandlings) which are found naturally in any heap of decaying organic matter and which are better known as fisherman's bait. They are small, red and wriggly, and are quite different from (though of course related to) the earthworm. They flourish in compost heaps and their appearance in the heap is one of the indications that the compost is about ready for use and that all is going well.

It is possible to create conditions in which a large proportion of the decomposition of organic matter is carried out by these worms rather than bacteria, fungi, etc. One system in use in this country was devised by Jack Temple and is described in the booklet *Worm Compost*, available from the Soil Association. It involves making a rather more complicated compost bin than the one described in this book, and also requires the regular addition of peat and calcified seaweed. It will compost all normal compost-heap materials in a- bout 6 months. The resulting compost will not be sterilized but will be a very rich product similar to worm castings.

The other method is American and is described in the book *Worms Eat My Garbage* by Mary Appelnorf, and is really only for recycling kitchen waste. As the book is probably hard to get in this country I will describe the process very briefly here: You make a wooden box (or preferably two) between 2 by 2ft by 8in (60 by 60 by 20cm) deep and 2 by 3 by 1ft (60 by 90 by 30cm) deep (depending on how much waste your household generates) and drill small holes in the bottom. You get 5lbs/2.2kg (for the 2 by 2ft box) to 10lbs/4.5kg (for the 2 by 3ft box) of bedding (shredded newspaper, soft cardboard, leafmould, peat or well composted manure), thoroughly dampen it and place it in the box. Put in your collection of brandling worms (about 100 is a good number to start with), keep the light on until they are driven down into the bedding (a few minutes) and then add your kitchen waste and cover it over with a piece of black plastic to keep the box moist. Continue to add kitchen waste as it becomes available, and add also an occasional dusting of ground limestone or calcified seaweed (don't use hydrated lime) as worms cannot survive in acid conditions. When the box is full, start again in the other box, using a trowel full or so of material from the first box to provide the starter worms for the second.

If you decide to try this worm compost and don't have your own supply of worms they can be bought at shops catering for fishermen.

I haven't tried this system and don't know anyone who has, but I understand that the Henry Doubleday Research Association are carrying out some trials.

Seaweed

Seaweed is one of the oldest organic fertilizers and has been in use in this country from remote times. It is still used extensively on commercial holdings in the Scilly Isles and Channel Islands. Its use in Cornwall has, alas, almost died out, through only 20 years ago I saw a compost heap of seaweed, sand, hedge trimmings and broccoli stalks as large as the largest haystack on a farm in Gulval. Seaweed contains less nitrogen and considerably more potash than farmyard manure and is therefore valuable for crops such as potatoes, peas, beans and tomatoes that benefit from potash. It is also especially valuable for globe artichokes, sea kale, asparagus and the beet family. If you apply it direct to the soil as a mulch it should be dug into the top few inches or covered with a sprinkling of earth, or it will dry very hard and brittle and be spread all over the place by birds and the wind. But it is probably best used in the compost heap because it is an excellent activator; it also provides a very wide spread of trace elements and minerals.

A great proportion of the U.K. lies within 40 miles of the coast and most people visit the seaside once or twice each year at least. It is really worth taking a few plastic bags to fill – gathering seaweed is quite enjoyable and when you get home its heady aroma, redolent of the seaside, will bring back happy memories – as well as being one of the best organic fertilizers there is. Don't keep it too long in closed bags, though, or it will deliquesce into a slimy mess which isn't very pleasant to handle, or to smell!

There are two main problems with seaweed. The first is its salt content. I think it is unlikely that you will ever use enough seaweed to endanger the salt level of your soil. The Scilly islanders and Cornish growers used seaweed as a fertilizer for centuries and maintained their soil in a high state of fertility. Worms, however, hate salt and cannot live in it, and I remember noticing on a visit to the Scilly Isles that the soil, fertile as it was, had extremely few worms in it. This might cause problems in certain situations or with growing systems that are very dependent on the activities of worms (for example, no-digging). It is possible in theory to wash the salt out of seaweed before using it and this is fine for people with a back yard and plenty of room but not so easy in the limited space of most houses.

The more serious problem with seaweed is radioactive contamination. I would definitely avoid gathering seaweed off the coast of Cumbria and in coastal areas washed by tidal waters from the vicinity of nuclear power stations. The map on page 120 shows the main tidal flows round the British Isles and the main sites of pollution.

Seaweed meal and liquid seaweed are manufactured products processed from seaweed that has been dried and ground. They are usually regarded as fertilizers and are dealt with on page 93.

Calcified seaweed is a very different product. It cannot be collected but has to be bought (see page 94).

No-Digging

Compost gardening has come to be associated with the no-digging technique, although of course compost can and should be used to advantage with any system of gardening. I do not really think this book is the right place to try to pronounce judgement on the digging versus no-digging controversy, and in any case I do not feel that there is any cut and dried answer. Generally speaking, I feel that the mistake made by most people is to think that there is just one all-embracing system of gardening that we must follow under all circumstances. Why should this be so? Soils differ; the climate differs; crops differ, our needs differ; the available technology changes. So also will systems vary to meet these varying circumstances and needs.

On sandy soils there is a need to build up the soil structure by incorporating organic matter. Continual disturbance of the soil would have the following consequences:

Increased aeration

Increased amount of oxygen in the soil

Increased bacterial activity

Increased break-down of complex organic molecules

Increased loss of energy in form of carbon dioxide

An increase of mineralization

A decrease in soil structure

A need for more compost

A decrease in the organic content of the soil.

In this case, therefore, the use of a no-digging technique could be generally beneficial in maintaining the organic content and soil structure.

The cycle of events shown above does incidentally demonstrate the fallacy of one widespread argument advanced against no-digging, which is that it requires such gargantuan quantities of compost that it is beyond the reach of ordinary mortals. This is the opposite of the truth. It is the continual disturbance of the soil and particularly of the lower layers that, by increasing the circulation of air, causes the organic matter to be dissipated. From this it is clear that if you have a limited amount of compost available, it is likely to be more economical to use this under a no-digging system than under a digging one.

The case of a pure clay is almost the opposite from that of a sandy soil. Here you are likely to have a soil structure already established: one component of this is a very complex network of cracks which are essential to root-formation. Disturb this and the structure will be broken up, and the soil will become compacted. On the other hand the long term improvement of a clay soil depends upon the incorporation of organic matter to a considerable depth in order to increase the granulation. So you have a choice, and as with many things in gardening it is difficult to lay down hard-and-fast rules. It is a matter of judgement, but unfortunately in this case there is very little knowledge on which to base this judgement.

What is surprising is that the original inconclusive experiment with comparative areas of digging and no-digging carried out by J. H. L. Chase nearly thirty years ago does not seem to have been repeated or followed up. So we are still lacking really sound practical evidence on which to judge the issue which is clouded with ignorance, fantasy and prejudice.

One essential for the no-digging technique is to encourage a large and flourishing population of worms who will be the best diggers of all, for they will carry surface organic matter down into the soil, digest it into a form that is suitable for incorporating into the soil, and maintain the soil structure by increasing the granulation.

Essential requirements for the worms are continuous supplies of organic matter, and a soil that is alkaline rather than acid. As plants, generally speaking, prefer a soil that is slightly acid, this means that you must take some care to keep your soil close to its optimum, neither too acid nor too alkaline. A pH of 6.5 (see page 94, 'Lime') or just over is the ideal balance, acid enough for plants and alkaline enough for the worms.

To keep the worm population thriving and well-fed it is a good idea to spread a layer of rather rough compost lightly over the area which the worms will gather up and take below the surface. Don't forget though that the same roughage is also attractive to slugs, so steps will have to be taken to discourage them! This use of organic mulches is particularly successful for bringing heavy clays into a workable condition. It takes several years but saves a lot of backache.

Buying In

Ideally the gardener should be able to make enough compost to improve and maintain the fertility of the soil indefinitely and for most soils it should not be necessary to buy any materials in from outside, with the possible exception of lime or calcified seaweed. However this is an ideal situation which may not be attained for several years; in the meantime compost may have to be supplemented and the question arises what is the 'best buy'. (See also Organic Fertilizers on pages 91-94.)

Manure

You can often buy this in bags at the roadside. If you really have trouble getting your heap to warm up it is worth buying a bag as an activator. For this it must be fresh; it must not have sawdust or chippings; it must not have too much straw; it should not be wet, and it should come from a reliable source; pig or chicken manure from intensive battery units should be avoided. Chicken manure from free range hens is the best of those likely to be available, with a nitrogen content almost twice that of cow or horse manure.

If you are buying manure for use direct on the garden you can either buy it already composted and 'well-rotted', which is simpler, or you can buy it fresh and compost it yourself which is probably better because most farmers are very careless about their manure heaps and allow half the goodness to be wasted. (See page 116.)

Peat

Peat is useful for potting compost; for seed beds; for storage of vegetables; for forcing chicory, etc. After such uses it will eventually find its way into the garden. It is inert, contains very little plant food, is usually very acid, and is not a very good buy for direct application to the garden. Particularly uneconomical are very often the 'cheap' bags you can buy at the roadside. Put your hand into these and you will be excited by the damp cool feeling and the peaty aroma. If you take it home and put a handful in a slow oven for a few days you'll wonder what has happened. Where has all that lovely damp peat gone? All you are left with is a tiny pile of dried-up brown stuff, which is the dry matter content of the handful of peat you put in originally. All the rest of the peat was water and has evaporated!

Here is an analysis of the water content of some typical peats:

	% *water*
Somerset sedge peat	89.2
Somerset peat (a brand name)	35.05
Irish sphagnum peat	49.3
Cumberland peat	65.6

What this means is that if you buy the Somerset sedge peat you are buying 9/10 water and only 1/10 peat, whereas with the sphagnum peat you are buying half water and half peat. To compare prices therefore the price of the Somerset peat must be multiplied by five.

If you have ever had experience of Irish sphagnum peat, you will know that it feels almost bone dry, so it is quite a surprise to learn that it is roughly 50 per cent moisture. Those cool damp dark peats by the roadside often have an even higher water content than the sample I measured, shown above, which was actually a reputable and well-known brand. If you buy peat which has a 95 per cent water content (not uncommon by any means) then you must multiply its cost by 10 to compare it with the cost of Irish sphagnum peat. Once you realize this you see that the roadside peat is not necessarily so great a bargain after all.

Compost

Exactly the same consideration applies of course to buying manure or compost or fertilizer, and it is always worth trying to find out or estimate the water content, so as to get an idea of the true price you are paying. I have seen some 'composted peat' products that were so sticky they must have contained well over 90 per cent water.

The second consideration in buying compost is to make sure it is compost and not a machine dried uncomposted mixture of sawdust and chicken manure from a battery where it may well be contaminated with insecticides that have been used in cleansing the battery house. If you buy mushroom compost make sure that it was made from horse manure and not from a chemical activator. Also it is wise to test its acidity as many mushroom composts are very alkaline which may be all right if your own soil is acid, but could be harmful if it is not. Many mushroom composts, too, are very strawy and if put on at once will inevitably lead to nitrogen starvation in your plants.

Some composts are 'fortified' with chemical fertilizers, so if you wish to be fully organic these should be avoided.

Leafmould

It isn't really worth buying in leafmould unless you are a keen grower of rhododendrons or azaleas or the like. But if you have an opportunity to collect it, it is as valuable as peat. For ecologically-minded people it has the advantage that it can be produced in one or two years and so it is not, like peat, a limited resource which is being exploited to effective extinction.

It is low in nitrogen and therefore useful when you want to increase the humus content of a soil without increasing its nitrogen content, e.g. for seedbeds. It should always be sieved as coarse wood chippings or beech-nuts, acorns, etc, would be detrimental (see nitrogen deprivation, page 63). Like peat it is useful for making potting compost – indeed it is the traditional base for this – but don't forget wherever you use it that it's likely to be very acid and this needs to be counteracted with lime or calcified seaweed.

Sewage Sludge

This is sold by some municipal authorities and is usually in the form of a fine dry powder. It is well-known for producing innumerable tomato seedlings but what is less understood is the possibility of its containing a dangerous level of heavy metals such as zinc, lead and cadmium. In industrial areas polluted waste is discharged into sewers which contaminates the sludge and as a result sewage sludge from some British works (e.g. London) does not meet the standards laid down by the E.E.C. – which are themselves likely to be made stricter in the near future. It is therefore not advisable to use sludge from industrial areas unless it is guaranteed to meet with E.E.C. standards. There is also a slight risk from pathogenic organisms, but sludge from rural areas should be safe to use providing you take two precautions: (1) Do not apply it to salad crops that are eaten uncooked; (2) Don't apply it within one month of harvesting a crop. It is a very good organic fertilizer and excellent to use in pea and bean trenches, or for potatoes and similar crops.

CONCLUSION

Throughout this book I have frequently made such remarks as 'although you may use a chemical, the convinced organic gardener would not do so.' How important is it that the compost gardener should be wholly and unequivocally organic? I do not think this question can at this stage be answered on a practical level or from experience; there just is not enough information or knowledge available. For that reason I do not recommend the use of either chemical fertilizers or pesticides if it can possibly be avoided. I do not think half enough is yet known of their ultimate effects on the soil or on our health. Mankind can hit the moon, split the atom, and blow the whole world to smithereens but we still have not begun to understand the forces at work in a teaspoonful of soil, and the ecology of a cubic yard of hedgerow is too complex for us.

These natural processes, which have taken millions of years to evolve, are affronted by mankind's arrogant belief that we can mould the whole universe to serve our own purposes. Within the brief space of our history we have already overreached ourselves a hundred times. Civilizations have fallen in ruins, the great cities of Ur and Babylon lie buried in the sands, the deserts creep relentlessly on. The bodies of every one of us contain increasing quantities of some of the deadliest poisons ever known. The peregrine falcon is almost extinct in these islands.

I am not suggesting that a packet of metaldehyde or a little nitrochalk are responsible for such dramatic disasters. But the acceptance of the doctrine that success lies with combating natural processes rather than co-operating with them contains dangers which are impossible to foresee; and the day of reckoning may be closer than we think.

WHAT IS ORGANIC?

Throughout this book I have used the word 'organic' rather loosely and I may have given the impression that all it implies is the use of natural composts, fertilizers and manures rather than synthetic or chemical ones and the avoidance of chemical and synthetic herbicides and insecticides. I think it is important to emphasize that this is only a small part of what is entailed in organic food production, the visible tip of the iceberg, as it were.

The organic movements both in this country and internationally have, over recent years, worked together to establish standards for organic food production that can be used to protect and promote the interests of both consumers and producers. The International Federation of Organic Agricultural Movements, which has membership in over 40 countries, has now drawn up a standards document to be used as a basis for national standards in membership countries. The British Organic Standards Committee has already agreed standards for Britain that comply with the International Federation's guidelines. These British standards are incorporated in a Symbol scheme that is administered by the Soil Association on behalf of the Committee. The Organic

Symbol is only awarded to, and can only be used by, producers who meet the British standards and producers are inspected regularly to ensure that they maintain the standards. The Scheme thus enables the general public to purchase genuine organically-grown produce, and protects both them and the producers against the marketing of so-called 'organically-grown' products that do not meet any accepted or identifiable standards.

The Scheme is thus intended to apply to commercial growers and farmers and is not, seemingly, directly relevant to private gardeners or smallholders but the standards it has set do provide guidelines against which gardeners can measure their own methods of cultivation.

The standards cover agriculture, horticulture and food processing and are rather detailed and lengthy. I have therefore set out below a resumé of the standards that seem to me to be most useful for gardeners. In some cases I have shortened or rearranged the text to make it more applicable to the gardener rather than to the commercial grower. Where I have interposed my own comments these are shown in italics.

In a few cases these standards do not agree with the practices I have recommended in this book. This is partly because they only became available after the book was passed to the publishers; it does not mean that I am in disagreement with them. However, sometimes the practices that are appropriate to professional market gardeners are different from those appropriate to the amateur and private gardener. Anyone who wishes for more detailed information about this or about farming standards should purchase the booklet 'Standards for Organic Agriculture', published by the Soil Association, 86-88 Colston Street, Bristol BS1 5BB for £5.00, post free.

Soil Association Standards For Organic Agriculture

1. Introduction

Organic (biological) agricultural and horticultural systems are designed to produce food of optimum quality and quantity. The principles and methods employed result in practices that:

- co-exist with, rather than dominate, natural systems
- sustain or build soil fertility
- minimize damage to the environment
- minimize the use of non-renewable resources.

The enhancement of biological cycles, involving micro-organisms, soil fauna, plants and animals is the basis of organic agriculture. Sound rotations, the extensive and rational use of manure and vegetable wastes, the use of appropriate cultivation techniques, the avoidance of fertilizers in the form of soluble mineral salts and the prohibition of agro-chemical pesticides form the basic characteristics of organic agriculture.

2. General Production Standards

Appropriate soil management is fundamental to successful organic production. The development and protection of optimum soil structure and fertility is the main goal of such management.

An optimum soil structure can be described as 'a water-stable, organic enriched, granular structure where all the water reserves within aggregates can be fully exploited by root hairs and the space between aggregates will be large enough to allow rapid drainage, to admit air and to facilitate the deep penetration of roots' (Elm Farm Research Centre: 'The Soil', 1984).

The development of such a structure relies partly upon natural physical and biological processes and partly upon soil management, which should ensure:

- regular input of organic residues
- a level of microbial activity sufficient to initiate the decay of organic materials
- conditions that ensure the continual activity of earthworms and other soil stabilizing agents
- as far as possible, a protective covering of vegetation, e.g. green manure or growing crop
- appropriate cultivations.

Mechanical cultivations can initiate rapid improvement in soil structure, although the effect will be temporary unless it is reinforced by structuring through biological activity. Appropriate cultivations should achieve:

- deep loosening of the soil
- minimal surface disruption
- timeliness to ensure appropriate tilth and to avoid damage to existing structure.

I am not clear how far the requirement for 'deep loosening of the soil' is in accord with the no-digging technique, which achieves the loosening of the soil principally by the encouragement of worm activity rather than by mechanical cultivation. I would argue for accepting no-digging in some conditions, though not necessarily in all. The standards have only just been issued and no doubt this and any other grey area will now be open to general discussion and clarification.

3. Rotations

It is recognized that the diversity of cropping and encouragement of predators, which is a feature of small intensive horticultural holdings, in part reduces the need for formal rotations. However, while there cannot be a definitive rotation, the following guidelines should be observed:

- a balance should be achieved between fertility building and exploitative cropping
- alternate deep-rooting crops with shallow-rooting crops
- alternate nitrogen-fixing and nitrogen-demanding crops
- alternate weed-susceptible and weed-suppressing crops
- Green manure, catch-cropping and undersowing should be utilized to ensure maximum soil cover
- Alliums (onions, etc.), brassicas and potatoes should not return to the same land until a gap of 48 months has elapsed from planting date to planting date.

I have considerable doubts as to whether it is practicable or even possible to practise the four-year rotation advocated in the last guideline in a small garden or allotment (see chapter 9 of my book Planning the Organic Vegetable Garden, *published by Thorsons Publishing Group, 1986).*

4. Manure

Bought-in manure should not, in general, form the basis of a manurial programme but should be an adjunct. *(This, however, is one of the requirements that* may be very difficult for the gardener, especially in the early stages of establishing a garden.) *The following should be avoided:

- bought-in manure from intensive poultry or animal sources
- mushroom compost that doesn't adhere to organic standards
- sewage sludge more than one year in three and then only on crops not for human consumption.

Excessive manuring should be avoided if it could give rise to a risk of nitrate contamination of water-courses or of nitrate levels in foodstuffs exceeding the recognized safety-limits already legally enforceable in some EEC countries. *(I don't think this is very likely to affect gardeners.)*

Composting is defined as a process of aerobic fermentation, reaching a temperature of up to 70°C (158°F). The material must be turned once and the heap should be maintained for at least three months.

I have to intervene here and say that I am a bit confused by this. Do the standards aim at a compost in which pathogenic microorganisms and weed-seeds, etc., are completely sterilized and destroyed? In this case, it would, I think, be better to say that a temperature of at least 60°C (140°F) should be reached. For full sterilization one turn is insufficient even if great care is taken to ensure that the outer 6 to 8in (15-20cm) of the old heap are turned into the centre of the new heap (by no means an easy feat in a small heap). For garden heaps at any rate, it is necessary to turn two or three times for complete sterilization in which case compost ready for use can be made in two months in the summer (or even less). I think it is better to depend on the quality of the end product rather than the length of time it has taken to produce it, which depends a lot on the raw materials, the climate, the season, the method used, and so on. If the standards are not aiming at a sterilized product, turning is not absolutely essential to producing acceptable compost, but various diseased and otherwise undesirable materials (as described on pages 41-42) should be specifically excluded.

I think it is probable that this instruction is aimed at farms rather than growers. With a large heap, or more properly stack, of strawed manure one turn may well be sufficient if it is carefully made and turned (see Plate 00). But I am surprised that more emphasis was not made on the necessity for keeping manure stacks under cover. Manure in the open will waste large amounts of its most valuable constituents. For example in experiments at Rothamsted Experimental Station, nitrogen losses after three months of composting were as follows:

- compact heap under cover: loss of 4 per cent nitrogen
- loose heap under cover: loss of 7 per cent nitrogen
- heap exposed in the open: loss of 33 per cent nitrogen.

5. Mineral fertilizers

Mineral fertilizers should be regarded as a supplement to and not a replacement for, nutrient recycling within the farm. A slow and balanced uptake of nutrients by the plant must be aimed for. In general, only fertilizers that release nutrients through an intermediate process, such as weathering or the activity of soil organisms, are allowed.

Single mineral or naturally occurring compounds are recommended. In the absence of more acceptable inputs, restricted use of soluble fertilizers to treat severe potassium or trace element deficiencies is allowed.

Use of the following fertilizers is approved (Note: I have omitted some approved materials that are not usually available in garden centres and so on):

- magnesium limestone (dolomite)
- calcium sulphate (gypsum)
- ground chalk
- limestone
- seaweed
- unadulterated seaweed foliar sprays
- calcified seaweed
- bonemeal
- fish meal
- hoof and horn meal
- wood ash
- dried blood
- wool shoddy
- hop waste
- sulphate of potash
- Epsom salts
- organic fertilizers bearing the Symbol.

All other mineral fertilizers are prohibited, including:

- nitrochalk
- Chilean nitrate
- urea
- muriate of potash
- kainit
- slaked lime
- quicklime
- proprietary organic fertilizers not bearing the Symbol.

6. Weed Control

Weeds can be seen as indicators of soil fertility and management practice. Many 'weed problems' are caused by imbalances in the management of the gardening system. The objectives of weed control within organic production is to suppress populations rather than eliminate them. Recommended control:

- Balanced rotations
- composting

- pre-sowing cultivations
- pre-germination, propagation, transplanting
- utilization of green manures and cover crops
- mulching
- mechanical operations, e.g., hand-weeding, hoeing, etc.

All chemical and hormone herbicides, both within the crop and along the edges, pathways and hedges of the garden, are prohibited.

7. Pest and disease control

This is primarily preventive rather than curative. The key factors are:

- hygiene
- rotational cropping
- balanced supply of plant nutrients
- creating an eco-system which encourages predators
- use of resistant varieties.

All synthetic pesticides and herbicides are prohibited. The following are allowed, though commercial producers have to obtain the Symbol Committee's approval for their routine use:

- pyrethrum
- derris
- quassia
- copper
- sulphur
- metaldehyde on non-cropping areas.

Post-harvest burning of straw, cereal waste and stubble is prohibited. *I suggest that for gardeners this should be extended to all garden waste with the exception of the non-compostible materials listed on pages 41-42.*
Where land is adjacent to land receiving herbicides there should be an effective wind-break to prevent spray-drift. This is an obvious precaution, though not always easy to achieve in gardens and allotments.

8. Horticultural systems

Conventional proprietary seed and potting composts are allowed until 1990 after which their nutrient supply must be organic. Conventional potted and non-potted plants and bare-root transplants are allowed until 1989, after which only organic ones are permitted. Peat, vermiculite, perlite, sand and untreated bark products are permitted.

I should emphasise again that the above resumé is only a short extract from a document that is 60 pages long. I have not set out in detail the strict controls that are applied to commercial producers. For example, a number of the materials and methods that I have shown as 'allowed' are in fact only allowed with the permission of, or under the supervision of, the Symbol Committee. As this does not apply to private gardeners, it seemed sensible to omit it, though of course it does enable one to distinguish between what can be done without qualification and what should only be done under certain conditions.

However, I think the above resumé gives a good idea of what organic gardening comprises, or should comprise: not merely the substitution of compost and organic fertilizers for chemical ones, but a whole system of overall organic management, every detail of which must be under scrutiny for the contribution it makes. It also demonstrates the very strict standards that commercial organic producers are expected to reach. There can be no doubt that produce carrying the Symbol will have been grown under prime conditions. Any other symbol, for example ones that merely proclaim 'OK

Organic' or 'Grown with Organic Fertilizers' should be treated with scepticism, if not suspicion.

As a matter of general interest, the EEC Commission is planning to introduce a directive that will eventually apply to the production and sale of all organically grown produce in member states. In addition, the Ministry of Agriculture, Fisheries and Food has established an organic working party whose brief is to report to the Minister and make recommendations on organic standards. It has in fact already issued proposals for a voluntary scheme that is less rigorous than the Soil Association Symbol Scheme and which seems unlikely to satisfy the organic movements in this country. There will no doubt be a period of discussion between the various bodies concerned, but it seems likely that within a short time it will become illegal to sell produce as 'organically grown' unless it carries a symbol of quality, authorized either by the EEC or by the government.

POLLUTION OF COASTAL WATERS

At first glance it does not appear that there is anywhere in the United Kingdom where it is safe to collect seaweed, apart, perhaps, from Northern Ireland and the western coast of Scotland. Tidal currents sweep right round our coastline carrying not only radioactive outfall but also large amounts of industrial waste containing poisonous substances such as lead and mercury. The fact is that the whole of Britain's coastline and its surrounding seas are polluted in one way or another and this is something we have to live with, but it is a matter of the degree of pollution and the danger it may be to health. I do not think the latter is known for sure and there is certainly no agreed consensus about it, but we do know, for example, that the amount of radioactive waste along the coastline near Sellafield, and the level of lead pollution in the Bristol Channel, are both dangerously high.

How much you are likely to be affected depends, of course, on how much seaweed you collect and how often you collect it. While regular collection could mean that cumulatively, you are exposed to dangerous levels of radiation, a one-off expedition may be harmless. I personally would avoid any area where there is a concentration of industrial waste discharge and dumping and any area close to a nuclear plant. This would include the Bristol Channel, Merseyside, the Clyde Estuary, the Firth of Forth, the Tyne, the Humber and the Thames Estuary. I would also avoid collecting from beaches that are swept by tidal currents that have passed nuclear outfalls within a distance of 20 miles, but I have to admit that these limits are a bit arbitrary – when I lived in Essex I was about 30 miles south of Sizewell and in that region where I found manure hard to come by and seaweed plentiful, I was reluctant to deprive myself of such a valuable composting material, and set my limits accordingly!

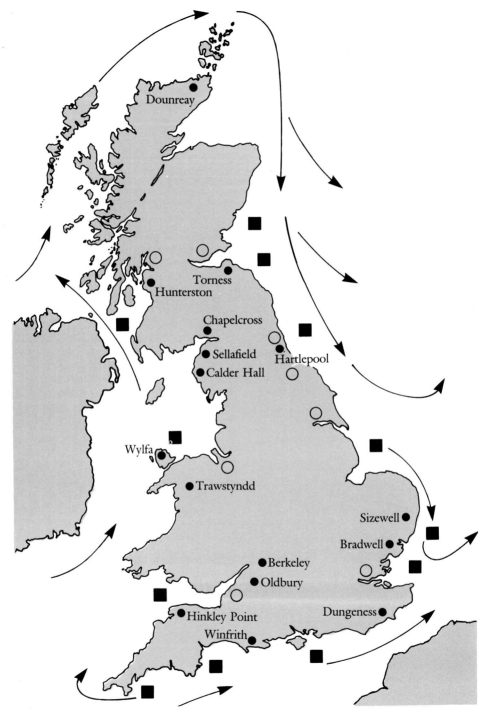

Dounreay

Torness
Hunterston

Chapelcross
Sellafield
Calder Hall
Hartlepool

Wylfa
Trawstyndd

Sizewell
Bradwell

Berkeley
Oldbury

Dungeness

Hinkley Point
Winfrith

● NUCLEAR POWER STATIONS AND REPROCESSING PLANTS

○ INDUSTRIAL WASTE DISCHARGE PIPES

■ INDUSTRIAL WASTE DUMPING SITES

← MAIN TIDAL CURRENTS

USEFUL INFORMATION

Organizations
Henry Doubleday Research Association, The National Centre for Organic Gardening, Ryton-on-Dunsmore, Coventry CV8 3LG (0203) 303517
The largest organic organization in the world. Provides a wide and invaluable range of services for the organic gardener, including advice, demonstration organic gardens, a mail-order business and a country-wide research facility. A must for all serious gardeners. Has several local groups.

The Soil Association, 86-88 Colston Street, Bristol BS1 5BB (0272) 290661
Originally mainly concerned with farming, but now very much directed towards smallholders. Has a number of local groups throughout the U.K. Operates the Organic Standards scheme, and Soilwatch, a scheme for monitoring soil erosion in the U.K.

WWOOF – Working Weekends on Organic Farms, 19 Bradford Road, Lewes, Sussex
Organizes weekends and longer stays on organic holdings for its members. Runs a training scheme for organic gardeners. Is an excellent entrée for beginners and can also provide a good introduction to the world of rural alternatives. Send a stamped addressed envelope for information.

Country College, 17 Burnbridge Road, Little Abington, Cambridge CB1 6BJ

(address your letter to Chris Mager)
Produces a correspondence course in organic gardening.

Friends of the Earth, 377 City Road, London EC1V 1NA (01-837) 0731
A widespread national and local pressure group, mainly concerned with environmental issues, but also with the provision of allotments and garden sharing schemes.

Suppliers
Chase Organics (U.K.) Ltd, Coombelands, Coombelands Lane, Addlestone, Surrey KT15 1HY
Sell a wide range of products for organic gardeners, including Chase Compost Seeds, which are guaranteed to be compost grown. Also green manure seeds, compost activators and seaweed products.

Henry Doubleday Research Association (address as above)
Sells a wide range of unusual seeds, including old-fashioned varieties, wildflower seeds and green manures. Also sells organic fertilizers, comfrey plants, compost activators and many other items for the gardener.

Further Reading
The Henry Doubleday Research Association has brought out a series of useful booklets on various topics.

The National Vegetable Research Station (now called the Horticultural Research Centre) has also brought out a number of leaflets. They are not confined to organic growing, but contain excellent advice which is backed by expert research. Their researchers have also produced two books (*Know and Grow Vegetables* I and II) which throw important new light on many aspects of vegetable growing. (National Vegetable Research Station, Wellesbourne, Warwickshire).

For a lot of information about the organic movement, and addresses of organizations, etc., there is *The Directory of Organizations and Training in the U.K. Organic Movement and Other Relevant Bodies* (published by WWOOF and available for £1.00 from WWOOF Mail Order, c/o Shoosmith, Lower Stainborough Fold Cottage, Barnsley, South Yorkshire S75 3HQ).

For almost everything you want to know about moving to the countryside and living there see *The Rural Resettlement Handbook*, available from Rural Resettlement Group, 55 Mint Road, Liss GU33 7DQ, price £4.95.

INDEX

The figures in bold type indicate main entries while those in italics indicate references to the colour Plates

acidity, **55**, 67, **94**, 108
activators, **49ff**, 61
  chemical 49
  'natural' 49-50
aeration,
  see compost heap, aeration
aerobic, **13ff**, 19, 20, 54
  method, **14ff**, 24, **40**, 51, 52, 53
Agriculture, Ministry of, 118
agro-chemicals, 9, 114
air, 13, 14, 40
  see also aerobic and compost heap, aeration.
alfalfa, *see* lucerne
anaerobic, **13**, 24
  method, 14, 15, **21ff**
Appelnorf, Mary, *Worms Eat My Compost,* 106
apple must, *see* must, apple
artichokes, Jerusalem, 77
  as green manure, 87

bacteria, 13, **14 (footnote)**, 15, 18, 62, **91, 92**
pathogenic, 21, 22
thermophilic, 20
bags, plastic, 37-39

beans, broad, 80-82, 85, 86
beans, field or tic, 81
blood, dried, 92
bone flour, 93
bone meal, 93
bonfire, 42
  ash, 40, *see also* woodash
bracken, 88, 93, 97
brandlings, 105, 106
brassicas,
  transplanting, *65,* 68, *96, 97,* 101
  stalks, 16, 42, 59
bristle, 72, 91
British Organic Standards Committee, 113

C/N ratio (carbon/nitrogen ratio), **16, 17,** 24, 41, 49, 59, 87
cabbage root fly, 65
calcified seaweed, *see* seaweed, calcified
California, University of, 50
carbon, 14, 15, 16, 17, 87, *see also* C/N ratio
carbon dioxide, 14, 15
carpet
  covering for compost heap, 22, 27
  mulch, *65, 96,* 99
carrots, sowing, 68
Chase, J. H. L., 108
Chase Organics, 123
chemical fertilizers, *see*

fertilizers, chemical
Chinese, 22, 50, 98, 104
clay soil, *see* soil, clay
clover, 87
comfrey, 49, 57, **87-88,** 102
compost,
  amount needed, **26ff**
  animal-free (veganic), 56
  buying in, 109
  definition of, 91, 115
  fresh, plants disliking, 68
  from battery houses, 109, 110, 115
  'nature's', 10, 11, 20
  quality of, 62, 63
  time spent making, 64
  use of, 67ff
compost area, **26ff,** *32,* 35ff
compost bin,
  bricks under, 18
  double bin, 27, 36
  construction of, **18ff, 29ff,** *32, 33*
  rotating of, 20
  siting of, 28
  size, 21, **26ff**
  slatted, 19
  temporary, 29
  wire mesh (wire netting), 18, 30
compost heap,